CW00349195

Rejoice O People

Rejoice O People

*Hymns and Poems
of Albert Bayly*

With an introduction to the man and his work
by David Dale

Nigel Lynn
Publishing & Marketing Ltd

2004

Published by Nigel Lynn Publishing & Marketing Ltd
on behalf of The Hymn Society of Great Britain & Ireland

Nigel Lynn Publishing & Marketing Ltd
106 High Street, Milton under Wychwood, Chipping Norton
Oxfordshire, OX7 6ET, United Kingdom

The Hymn Society of Great Britain & Ireland
The Honorary Secretary, 99 Barton Road,
Lancaster, LA1 4EN, United Kingdom

This compilation copyright © The Hymn Society
of Great Britain & Ireland 2004

First published 2004

All rights reserved. No part of this publication may be reproduced, stored in a retrieval system, or
transmitted, in any form or by any means, without the prior permission in writing of The Hymn
Society of Great Britain & Ireland, or as expressly permitted by law, or under terms agreed with
the appropriate reprographic rights organisation. Enquiries outside the scope of the above should
be addressed to The Hymn Society at the address shown

This book must not be circulated in any other cover or binding and this same condition must be
imposed on any acquirer

The words of the hymns, poems and sonnets in this book are covered by the
Christian Copyright Licensing Scheme, PO Box 1339, Eastbourne,
East Sussex, BN21 4YF, United Kingdom

British Library Cataloguing in Publication Data
Data available

ISBN   0 9505589 5 8

1 3 5 7 9 10 8 6 4 2

Typeset in Plantin by
Nigel Lynn Publishing & Marketing Ltd

Cover design by Wheeler & Porter Ltd, Banbury

Printed in the United Kingdom
on acid-free paper by
Antony Rowe Ltd, Chippenham

Contents

Foreword

TWENTY years after his death, Albert Bayly lives on in hymn books all over the world. However, most of Albert's 180 hymns and 62 poems now appear only in his own booklets which are out of print, so I visited the Pratt Green Library at Durham University to see the entire collection which is lodged there. I soon realised that many of the hymns are as relevant to today's world as they were in Albert's lifetime, such was his great gift of vision, a man before his time—and his poems, especially those about his beloved Thaxted, are a sheer delight.

A plan in the late 1980s to publish Albert's entire output, together with essays on his life and work by his friend, David Dale, never reached fruition. An author acknowledged as 'the father of modern hymn writing' surely deserves a lasting memorial, and I am delighted that The Hymn Society of Great Britain & Ireland has agreed to publish this selection of hymns and poems, together with a revision of the essays.

Thanks are extended to:

David Dale for his preparation of the book that failed to appear

Dick Watson for editing and updating David Dale's essays

Alan Gaunt for selecting the best hymns and poems

Sheila Hingley and her staff at Durham University Library for their co-operation

The Hymn Society for taking responsibility for the work

The Pratt Green Trust for financial assistance

Nigel Lynn for undertaking the publishing

VALERIE RUDDLE

May 2004

Acknowledgements

Poems, sonnets & hymns by Albert Bayly (1901-84)
© 1988 Oxford University Press.
Reproduced by permission. All rights reserved.
The words of the hymns, poems and sonnets in this book are covered
by the Christian Copyright Licensing Scheme.
For reproduction outside the scope of the scheme, please contact:
Music Copyright Administrator, Oxford University Press,
Great Clarendon Street, Oxford, OX2 6DP, United Kingdom
Telephone +44 (0)1865 353289   Fax +44 (0)1865 353749
E-mail music.permissions.uk@oup.com

Albert Bayly   1901–1984

Albert Bayly
The Man and his Ministry

No MORE fitting description could be given of this totally dedicated minister of the Gospel and very complete human being than these lines from his own poem in praise of his beloved Thaxted, where he lived from 1962 to 1972:

> …The grace of quiet lives
> bright with the beauty of true holiness.

When Albert Bayly was invited in his retirement to become honorary associate minister at the United Reformed Church in Chelmsford, the minister observed that they did themselves an honour in asking him and thus formally recognising his ministry in that church. That was no empty praise. For Albert had behind him a life of ministry singularly marked by grace and godliness. He was also well known beyond the churches in which he served, as a hymn-writer of distinction. But it was primarily as a man of quiet grace and true holiness that he was known and loved by the people of Chelmsford and almost certainly also by those others who, in former years, had benefited from his ministry.

Albert was born into a church-going Congregational family on 6 September 1901 at Bexhill-on-Sea in Sussex. His father had two sons by a previous marriage, Haswell and Sidney. Albert was the eldest child of the second marriage, with a brother, Edward Francis, and sister, Dorothy. He went to school at Bexhill and later to Hastings Grammar School. He left school at 15 and, after passing a Civil Service examination, was able to enter as a naval boy shipwright at the Royal Dockyard School at Portsmouth. He later entered the Dockyard itself as a 'docky' and apprentice. Here he worked for eight years and gained wide experience of different kinds of work, including time in the carpentry department and in the drawing office. He always spoke with a simple pride of his experiences in Portsmouth. They gave him an understanding of everyday life, and he was as much at home with working people as he was with the colleagues he came to know at Mansfield College, Oxford, or later in his ministry in the Church. Like the Apostle Paul, he was not ashamed—indeed he was proud—of having worked with his hands.

Slowly but surely, during this time in the Dockyard a conviction was growing within him that he should offer himself for the Christian ministry. He received much help and guidance from the Revd. Henry Parnaby, minister of Buckland Congregational Church, who advised him to work for an external Bachelor of Arts degree of London University as preparation for theological training. This he did through a correspondence course involving intensive study at home when his work at the Dockyard was done. It was no easy assignment, for work at the Dockyard began at 7am, and it must have required great self-discipline and determination to apply himself to his books after a hard day's work. He learned Latin vocabulary while pushing his cycle up the hills to and from his work. Later, when called upon to coach students who were preparing for lay preaching or auxiliary ministry, his mind must often have returned to his early discipline of study. If his students felt at times that he was a hard task-master (he would tolerate no sloppiness of thought or practice), they also knew that he had a sympathy born out of hard experience of extra-mural study.

In 1924, Albert gained his hard-won degree. In the following year he applied for entry to Mansfield College, the Congregationalists' theological college in Oxford. The College was not a recognised College of the University, and Albert was required to matriculate as a member of St Catherine's Society, at that time the method of entry to the University for Mansfield students. He began his studies in the Michaelmas Term of 1925, and entered very fully into the life of the College. Until pressure of studies made him give up, he was a member of a rowing eight, and he made a number of life-long friends during his time there. Among them was Eric Shave, who later brought his musical gifts to a fruitful collaboration with Albert in his hymn-writing activities. Mansfield meant much to him throughout his life. For some years he was Editor of the Mansfield College Magazine, and he wrote several poems for particular occasions in its recent history.

During his time at the Dockyard, Albert had for four years attended the Royal Dockyard School for two afternoons and three evenings a week. Here the emphasis had naturally been on scientific training. This interest in scientific studies never left him. In Oxford he made full use of the opportunity to attend the British Association meetings where he listened with great interest to speakers like Sir Arthur Eddington on astronomy (he had been fascinated by astonomy from an early age), Sir Oliver Lodge on spiritualism, and Sir Leonard Woolley on biblical archaeology. His interest in practical religion continued too: from Mansfield, he went to Westhill College, Selly Oak, Birmingham, for a three-week course on Sunday School and Youth Work for theological students. This was at a time when Dr George Archibald, the pioneer of graded schools, was principal.

On 19 August 1928, Albert began his ministry at Fairway Hall, Monkseaton, Northumberland. It was a small daughter church of the Whitley Bay Congregational Church, where Albert was ordained on 18 March 1929. It had been at one time a Wesleyan Methodist Chapel, 'built in 1843', says Mr W.W. Tomlinson in his historical notes on Monkseaton, 'by the village grocer, shoemaker and blacksmith and two labouring men'. The Wesleyans left the building in 1913 for larger premises in the town, and in 1921 the building became the property of a Monkseaton resident who converted it into a hall for village purposes. In 1927 the building was taken over by the Whitley Bay Congregational Church and, with the help of local preachers of many denominations, Sunday services were resumed. Twelve months later, Albert was appointed as Assistant Minister of Park Avenue Congregational Church under the Revd A.S. Evans, with special responsibility for Fairway Hall. This was an arrangement made possible through the generosity of a local philanthropist and man of quiet missionary zeal, Henry B. Saint.

Noel Kilby, a life-long friend of Albert, was a boy of 14 when Albert came to Fairway Hall. He was seconded from Park Avenue to play the piano in the Sunday School, later becoming a teacher there. He writes:

We knew him first as a shy, almost awkward man: dedicated to his work, an enthusiast for missionary work which he would dearly have liked to undertake himself. He trained many of us as teachers, lay preachers and workers in different fields: at that time we did not appreciate the devoted work, the meticulous attention to sermon preparation, the blending together of all parts of his services to make them a unity, the painstaking pastoral duties which must have been agony for one so reserved. My wife recalls how, when she was 16, she had appendicitis, and was visited by Albert when she came home from a nursing home. He sat on a chair at the side of the bed; conversation was difficult; he seemed uneasy; only when he had gone did she discover that she had placed a prickly hairbrush face up on the chair, and Albert had been too shy to say anything, enduring the discomfort the whole of the visit.

In a message to his church on the tenth anniversary of their existence as a Congregational Church and his ninth as minister, Albert spoke of the range of activities and the variety of service being offered by the church, and then went on:

Personal prayer and disciplined living are prime necessities. We must constantly turn to God and seek his will for us and for our Church. We must give God the first claim upon our time, our thought, our energies.

We must study our Bible and especially the New Testament, individually and together, to discover afresh what God has to say to us and to our generation. We must test all our Church activities by the contribution they make towards building God's Kingdom of Christ-like human lives. We must found our fellowship with one another on deeper understanding and Christian sympathy. And we must be alert to the new circumstances of our age, with the demand they make for wider conceptions of Christian service and new methods of presenting the old message.

This represents a fair summary of Albert's convictions about the church's priorities, not just at this time but also throughout his life. His sense of the importance of prayer, Bible-study and self-discipline was balanced by an equally strong sense of the relationship between the church and the world.

It was here at Fairway Hall that Albert met his first wife, Marjorie Shilston, a member of St James' Church, Newcastle. They married and worked together in Monkseaton before moving to Morpeth, still in Northumberland, in 1938. A year later, just as they were settling in to their work there, the Second World War began. Not only did this disrupt the pattern of church activities and take away some of the congregation on active service, but it also revealed the strength of the minister's beliefs. Albert was a convinced pacifist, and at one point he found his diaconate remonstrating with him for holding pacifist meetings in the manse. It was typical of Albert that he listened to what was being said before quietly expressing his own convictions about war and peace. He was never aggressive, but always totally consistent, and unshakable in his beliefs. His stance on pacificsm, however, did not prevent him from forming relationships with troops stationed in the Morpeth area. Marjorie and he regularly entertained soldiers stationed in the district, sharing their meagre rations with the young men, who were often far away from their own homes and families. It is said that on one such occasion, Albert and Marjorie, after giving hospitality to their new-found friends, ran out of food completely and had to make do with porridge for a weekend. Many of the friendships made in those years were maintained until the time of his death.

Albert's ministry was always quiet but deeply personal and pastoral. On his death, a letter came from one who had been with them in those war years at Morpeth, expressing sympathy and also telling a story:

> We had the great sadness to lose a little four-year-old boy through illness. Albert conducted the funeral and was a great help and support to our family. On the first anniversary of David's death in May 1942, Albert wrote to us and every year since we received a letter from him. In May 1965 my husband died. However, the letters concerning the two events still came without a break until May this year. I realise that the last one has now been written and am saddened by this fact. I am sure that we were not the only family for whom Albert performed this service but it lasted 42 years and for this and many happy occasions ... my family and I will always treasure his memory.

Mention has already been made of Albert's interest in the work of the Church overseas. He would dearly have loved to have given himself to that work but it was judged that his health would not stand up to a tropical climate. This did not prevent his missionary interests finding an outlet in other ways. He became a Director of the London Missionary Society, serving for many years on the East Asia Committee and also on the Pilot Committee (an organisation for encouraging missionary interest and support in children and young people). Albert was much involved in the LMS. Triple Jubilee Celebrations (1795–1945) and, as Honorary Secretary of the District Auxiliary, was caught up in the outworking of those celebrations in Northumbria. It was for these celebrations that Albert wrote his first hymn, *Rejoice, O people, in the mounting years*, set to a tune by Eric Shave. It first appeared in a Northumbrian souvenir booklet of the Triple Jubilee called *Faith's Transcendent Dower* (a phrase from a Wordsworth sonnet, which would have delighted Albert).

The war ended in 1945. A year later the Baylys moved from Morpeth to Hollingreave, Burnley, Lancashire. Here grief and joy were strangely blended. It was here that Marjorie, his wife and helpmate over many years, died. After some time Albert met and later (July 1950) married Grace Fountain, who was a Home Missionary in charge of the Westgate Church at the other end of the town. It was a good marriage. Grace brought to the partnership her loving support and ministerial experience, but she also drew out of Albert a sense of humour which had largely been dormant. They worked hard in both church and community, being keen workers for social service and for International Voluntary Service for Peace campaigns. This organisation was involved in a variety of voluntary activities, from helping old people with their gardens, to the reconstruction, for use of refugees, of a burnt-out mansion in Carclew, Cornwall. Albert also worked for some time in marriage guidance.

His carol *If Christ were born in Burnley* was written for use as a Christmas card for his friends in the church. It is said to have been inspired by the adjacent moorland but it is difficult to avoid the thought that it might also have been suggested by the celebrated piece by the poet-priest Geoffrey Studdert-Kennedy,

If Jesus came to Birmingham. For these were not the happiest years of Albert's ministry.

Pastorates followed at Swanland, a Yorkshire village near Hull (1950–56), and Eccleston, a suburban church on the outskirts of St Helens, Lancashire, (1956–62). It was in the early 1950s that the missionary calling stirred again. A minister was required for work in Johannesburg. Albert offered his services and this time passed the medical examination. However, a person on the spot was found and Albert remained in Britain.

It was about this time that Albert began the publication of his hymn collections. *Rejoice O People* appeared in 1950, with 55 hymns and poems. In the introduction Albert said that 'it was the unexpected interest shown in the hymn *Rejoice, O people* which encouraged me to attempt others'. It was the beginning of thirty years of hymn writing. The publication of this first booklet, and the four others which followed, paved the way for the inclusion of some of his work in major hymn-books throughout the English-speaking world. He also produced poems and sonnets for special occasions and as greetings to friends at Christmas time. At one stage he wrote missionary plays and demonstrations for the children and young people in the churches where he served. The words and style of these are now largely outmoded, but they display a keen concern that young people should be quickened by his own love of the Church and loyalty to the Gospel.

Albert was brought up in the days of the great pioneer missionaries and before the present ambivalence about overseas missionary activity had set in. Kendall Gale was one of the last of the missionary pioneers who, after a successful ministry in this country, went to Madagascar in 1908 to take up the work laid down by a friend who had died. Albert greatly admired his work and character. In 1960 his biography of Kendall Gale appeared, published by the London Missionary Society. This was in one sense a follow-up to his hymn, *Lord of all gallant hearts*, written in 1947 for the missionary celebration, *A Whirlwind for Christ*, commemorating the life of Kendall Gale, also published by the London Missionary Society. The book is a fascinating account of the church being planted and growing in Madagascar, based upon letters home from Kendall Gale himself and from visiting officials from the Missionary Society. The book speaks of an age and style of churchmanship at home and overseas that ministers of today, and indeed for the greater part of Albert's day, might envy but scarcely emulate. Its interest at this point is the way in which it paints a clear picture of one who was perhaps a mirror-image of what Albert might have wished to be: a large, cheerful extrovert, a strikingly successful evangelist. They had this in common, that they were both, in their different ways, pioneers, and both had a passionate desire to make known the saving power of Jesus Christ and an unswerving loyalty to the Kingdom.

It was during his years at Eccleston that Albert delivered a memorable address to the Liverpool District Council of the Lancashire Congregational Union, entitled *Forty Years On*. It began:

> 'Forty years on' will bring the early years of a new century. It requires us to look ahead only a little longer than I can look back as a minister. It gives us a convenient vantage point from which to look at the Church as it could become if we heed the calls that I believe God is presenting to us today.

In that paper, which stirred considerable interest and discussion, Albert presented his vision of a 'Reformed Church of Christ' in England that embraced the former Free and Established Churches. He made plain that what he was looking for was not a monolithic, monochrome structure but a united church to which each tradition brought something of value and gained something from the others; in which there was 'variety in ways of worship and local organisation, but a deep sense of belonging to one family in Christ, and of presenting to the world a single fellowship ruled by one Lord'. There is no dating of this paper but it is likely that it was in the early sixties (Albert left Eccleston in 1962) and was certainly before the memorable Nottingham Conference of Churches in 1964, when the call to unity was so strongly sounded.

Albert presented his hope in the form of a dream, in which the United Church came into being in 1985 'after many years of negotiation and discussion'. He described being taken into a sanctuary impressive in its simple beauty:

> In shape it was two semi-circles, a larger and a smaller one, joined along a common diameter. The larger one was set with chairs, not pews, for the congregation. The smaller one formed a semi-circular apse, which contained the communion table and pulpit.

This suggests that he had by this time lost any love he might have once had for the old Victorian preaching centres, much as he still believed in the preaching of the Word.

Turning to the combined hymn and service book provided in the sanctuary, he wrote:

> I noted some familiar hymns and psalms, along with many hymns new to me in which various aspects of contemporary life were offered to God, the sciences and arts, the affairs of home, daily work and leisure, of world government and the universal Church. The music of the voluntary which was now being played on an organ of manifestly fine quality, which inspired devotion, struck me as the creative expression of a new and exciting age.

It is interesting that while Albert foresaw many of the later developments in Church life—greater congregational participation in worship with more time for free and spontaneous prayer, tea or coffee after service, growth of the house-church movement, greater social and political concern on the part of the churches, and the possibility of new forms of hymn-writing—he did not envisage the singing of choruses, so much part of a certain type of evangelistic worship today. The one hymn that he recorded as being sung in his vision was by John Ticehurst, which begins:

> O God of office, desk and stool,
> Of drawing board and typing pool,
> Of every shop and store ...
>
> (*Rodborough Hymnal* 71)

It was typical of the man that whilst he rejoiced in the great tradition of the Church, he was always looking ahead and trying to grasp the vision which the Risen Christ had for his people. The great commission remained: 'Go therefore and make disciples of all nations ...'

After six years in Eccleston, Albert felt that his work there was done and asked for a pastorate in the South of England. This was the only time he made any request about stationing. As Grace's family and his own were in the South, it made sense to seek an appointment that would then, and in his retirement, bring them closer together. Accordingly, they moved to Thaxted, Essex, in 1962. This was perhaps 'the jewel in the crown' of Albert's ministry. It lasted for ten years, which carried it well beyond the normal retirement age. There was something about the quality and character of this country town, with its historic buildings, its societies, its culture and its people, that attracted his painter's eye, quickened his poetic sensibility, and caused him to speak of Thaxted, in both his conversation and poetry, with tremendous love. It was a continuing source of pleasure to him that the manse at Thaxted had been the home of Gustav Holst.

His work there, as in other places, was quietly unspectacular. Albert was not one who sought the headlines. His job, he knew, was to minister, not just to register. He had no time for the evanescent, for any appeal to the mood of the moment, or for any form of outward show. Here, as elsewhere, he was known and valued for his friendship, his pastoral care, his faithful preaching, and his careful conduct of worship. He established good ecumenical relationships with the Roman Catholics, but attempts to work with other local churches did not always meet with the success that he would have liked. It was, however, a good ministry and a fitting conclusion to his itinerant career. He was a man of many interests and talents and very much involved in the life of the community. He was a keen gardener: he liked working with his hands and maintaining his contact with God's good earth. He enjoyed walking, with its opportunity of taking in the beauty of nature in all its forms. His painting, always a joy to himself and others, probably came to full expression during those Thaxted years.

In 1972 Albert and Grace moved to a newly-established retirement home in a small house in the Springfield area of Chelmsford, some twenty miles from Thaxted. Albert later confessed that he and Grace did not know how they would settle there. They were a couple of miles out of the town. There was no Congregational Church (the URC was formed later that year) in Springfield. Christ Church, the main Congregational/URC church, was nearly three miles away. They had no car and bus services on Sunday were infrequent, to say the least. They were both keen walkers but did not know how they would be able to be full members of the church community at such a distance. However, they soon found that there was no lack of friends to take them to church by car when they required this. They quickly established themselves and became valued members of the Church community.

Not all retired ministers settle comfortably in another's church. But Albert's ministerial experience, his forward-looking stance, his world-wide vision, his self-effacing and caring nature and his generous self-giving , were widely valued and he was soon invited to become Honorary Associate Minister of the Church (it was at this time that the minister described the church as honoured as it formally recognised his ministerial function). He took this as a further call to service and one to which he devoted much time and energy. In this role, which in so many ways Grace shared with him, (at one time both were members of the Eldership), Albert was highly regarded by ministers, elders and members. He was a man of prayer who maintained his hold of God by persistent attention to the means of grace. It was not for nothing that he was asked to look after the mid-week prayer meeting at Christ Church. His life was manifestly shot through with prayer. It was this that enabled him to sit with people in both joy and sorrow and share the experience to the utmost because he also shared it with God.

He was a man of praise and the key-note of his hymn-writing was one of rejoicing in God. Like the prophet Isaiah, he had in his early days caught a vision of the Lord in glory. For him the bush had burned and not been consumed. That delight in God, so rarely spoken of in our day, was a major part of his inspiration behind his painting, his poetry and his particular stance in life. He was also one who knew that the essential task of a preacher of the Gospel is to be prepared to say in word and deed, 'Thus saith the Lord'. Though quiet and unassuming in all that he did, Albert was not afraid to wear the prophet's mantle. One of the members of his former church at Burnley said of him:

> He was very intellectual. Sometimes he seemed to be in a world of his own. But he was very much down to earth. He knew what was going on.

Yes, he knew what was going on, in the Church and the world, and was not afraid to offer a quiet word of rebuke, if that was what was required. There were neighbours in Chelmsford who, having brought their church membership 'lines' from Scotland, having had their child baptised at Christ Church and been much encouraged by Albert and Grace, just fell away. When Albert asked why they did not attend the Church, the wife made some excuse about being too busy. Albert said quietly and sadly, 'I'm disappointed.'

His was no cloistered faith: it was constantly being worked out in the life of the Church and the life of the world. It was no conservative faith: it was a living, growing faith, ever open to new possibilities of interpretation and understanding. In her address at the Funeral Service in Chichester, Kate Compston, one-time assistant minister at Christ Church, spoke of Albert as a kind of Renaissance man: 'clearly appreciating, and intrigued and excited by, scientific discovery, and always looking for new ways of communicating his wonder over scientific achievement in poetic language—trying to bring the disciplines together, realising that religion embraces both, sees all life ultimately as one ... and helping others to that wonder too.'

His was not a conventional faith. It carried with it an element of risk and adventure; a quest for what God is saying to us, in and through the events of contemporary life. He saw clearly that the righteousness and the love of God has to be seen throughout the paradoxes and the problems, the ambiguities and the anxieties, the sins and the sufferings of the present time. In this connection it is worth recalling the words of his hymn which begins:

> Our God, whose love in anger burns
> At every human wrong;
> When cruel men oppress the weak
> And glorify the strong.
> (*Rejoice Always* 12)

A fellow member of Christ Church wrote of him:

> Albert was a re-assurance to me at the more hazardous range of my

adventures in discipleship. He was the Vice-Chairman of the Chelmsford Amnesty Group, and his contribution to its periodic debates about how best (or even whether) to support a particular prisoner were clear-sighted and generous. Weather rarely kept him away from a meeting ... But it was particularly in the matter of the Peace Tax Campaign that I valued his judgement ... This was new ground to me, and I was thankful that Albert had trodden it first.

This same friend wrote also of the occasion when Albert, at the age of 81, braved a heavy downpour to join an extremely muddy sponsored walk: 'He was by no means the last to arrive.'

The last years of his life were made more difficult by failing sight. Albert had begun to suffer from glaucoma during his time in Thaxted. He subsequently had an operation on each eye. This left him with one good eye and the other less than good. In Chelmsford he suffered a blood clot in the better eye and this resulted in almost complete loss of sight. All his reading had to be done for him. Grace spent time every day helping him to keep up with the news and with general reading. Other friends read books on to tapes to which he listened. For nearly three years he patiently bore with this limitation of sight, maintaining his work at the Church as best he could, doing his allotment gardening and providing oversight for lay preacher training. He did confide to Grace at the time 'if it were not for leaving you, I wouldn't mind dying, for I have done all I wanted to do.'

During this difficult period he wrote his hymn, *The Inner Vision* (*Rejoice in God* 25), see page 110, beginning 'I have seen beauty in the hills', and continuing in the second verse:

> When age dims outward sight, give me, O Lord,
> that inner vision which few can see, within,
> the beauty hidden from the outward eye ...

It was partly an outpouring of gratitude for all that life had given but also a prayer for an even richer, and more heavenly, vision.

Some two years later, in 1979, he went into Chelmsford and Essex Hospital and had an operation for cataract. He wrote movingly about that experience in *Rejoice Together* (Part 1, 22), see page 115. From this time on Albert's sight improved and, despite a remark made to him by the late Nathaniel Micklem (one-time Principal of Mansfield College) that the muse does not visit those who are over eighty years old, Albert went on to produce a hymn for an Anglia Television Easter Hymn Competition, *Life is born of death today*, with a tune composed by Michael Dawney. They were awarded runner-up prize and the hymn was included in the Television Broadcast.

Albert and Grace had always regarded the annual conference of The Hymn Society of Great Britain and Ireland as a high point in their year. They had attended regularly for nearly twenty years. It was particularly fitting that the business in 1984 included review sessions on the Methodist *Hymns and Psalms* (1983), which contains no less than twelve of Albert's hymns. After the conference, Albert and Grace had intended visiting friends in the Seaford area, but on the day following its conclusion, Albert suffered a heart attack and died shortly afterwards (26 July). A funeral service was held in Chichester conducted by the

Revd Kate Compston, a former minister of Christ Church. This was followed by a Service of Thanksgiving at Christ Church, Chelmsford, on 12 October when tributes were paid to his work as hymn-writer by Caryl Micklem and to his life and ministry by David Dale. But, as the writer of the tribute in the Hymn Society *Bulletin* observed: 'Unwittingly he provided his own epitaph in writing his well-known lines based on Micah 6. 8, "What doth the Lord require ... do justly; love mercy; walk humbly with thy God", for in Albert precept and practice were indistinguishable.'

In response to a friend who expressed sympathy on hearing of Albert's death, Grace wrote, 'Albert died as he had lived, quietly and peacefully. He always had that calm and inner peace, plus the Christian hope of a better world here and the world beyond this. [He was] a man of prayer, which he never neglected, whatever the circumstances.'

His message remains:

> Rejoice, O people, in the days to be,
> when, o'er the strife of nations sounding clear,
> shall ring love's gracious song of victory.

Albert Bayly
The Man and his Writing

The man and his themes

RELATIVELY few people knew Albert Bayly as a man; some hundreds knew and valued him as a Christian minister; many thousands on both sides of the Atlantic, in Australia and in New Zealand, know of Albert Bayly, the hymn writer. Those who knew him as friend or minister recognised that the same man appeared as the hymn writer. There was a certain wholeness about his personality, so that though different people might see different facets of Albert Bayly, they always knew that it was the same person shining through them all. There was an essential identity and integrity that marked everything he did.

His first hymn, *Rejoice, O people, in the mounting years*, was written in 1945. The story of its composition is best told in his own words, spoken at a meeting of the London Branch of the Hymn Society on 27 January 1968:

> It was really the Triple Jubilee of the London Missionary Society. It was the occasion that moved me to try. I was helping in the production of a little booklet on Tyneside, the history of the Newcastle-on-Tyne Auxiliary of the LMS and I was feeling quite moved by the occasion and thought I would have a shot at it and then I found that I could do so.

> It might have just ended there except that I did have some copies—loose

sheets of the hymn, with the original tune which Eric Shave did—on sale in the Livingstone House Book Room, and Cyril Taylor came along and evidently was browsing through the Book Room and happened to pick up one of these sheets and seemed to be interested in it and wrote to me, because he was concerned with producing the BBC book at that time and asked me if I would revise the hymn as it was too specialised for use as it stood—revise it for the BBC book.

Well, of course, this was a great surprise to me and a great encouragement. I did revise it and then Dr. Iremonger, the Dean of Lichfield, was celebrating the 750th anniversary of the Cathedral and he was on the same committee and asked if I would write a special verse for Lichfield. That was how the third verse came to be written, which gave it six long verses. But the third verse is not integral to it and can be used where appropriate. So that is how it came to be written and to be in the BBC book. Then, of course, *Congregational Praise* got interested in it and Dr. Thiman wrote his tune. Then I thought, having tried once, I would try again.

The additional verse written for Lichfield Cathedral recalls Albert's pride in his time at Portsmouth Dockyard, and his awareness of good craftsmanship. It celebrates not only the lives of the saints but also the beauty of the cathedral building and the skill of the workmen who built it:

> Rejoice, O people, in the deathless fame
> won by the saints whose labours blessed our land;
> and those who wrought for love of Jesus' name
> with art of builder's and of craftsman's hand.
>   Rejoice in him whose Spirit gave the skill
>   to work in loveliness his perfect will.

> (*Rejoice Together* Part 2, 1) see page 2

The response of Cyril Taylor and the intervention of the Dean of Lichfield were of great importance in encouraging Albert to go on writing. He was so modest that, as he said, 'this was a great surprise to me', but during the next few years he wrote hymns when he could find the time. In the introduction to his first collection he said 'It is not easy for a working minister to devote himself without interruption to this kind of activity. Many of these lines have been thought out and jotted down walking along the street, in the bus [he never owned a car and did the greater part of his visiting on foot], or at odd moments between ministerial engagements.' At first he wrote for particular occasions. He welcomed the foundation of the World Council of Churches in 1948 with the visionary *Seen at Amsterdam 1948*:

> I saw a city come from God above,
>   of beauty pure and rare:
> a bride adorned for Christ her husband's love,
>   in garments rich and fair …

> I see her beauty in the eager eyes
>   of consecrated youth;
> and mirrored in the features of the wise
>   behold her heav'nly truth.

> (*Rejoice Together* Part 2, 45) see page 26

In the same year he recorded the bicentenary of Isaac Watts (1674–1748), using the metre of the 148th Psalm in the 'Old Version', 66.66.4444, which Watts himself knew and loved. Each verse begins with a recognition of the glory of God:

> Thy glory moved the heart
> of sacred bard to sing,
> with consecrated art,
> his praise to heaven's King …
>
> (*Rejoice Together* Part 2, 18) see page 14

Also noteworthy is the series of seventeen hymns on the Old Testament prophets. It was part of his conviction that the Bible, and changing interpretations of it, must be taken into account by the hymn writer. In the preface to *Rejoice O People* he acknowledged the debt he owed to Bernard Manning for this, and went on: 'I have realised what a wealth of Biblical material remains to be drawn upon by hymn writers, if one may judge by our present hymn books.' Without in any way diminishing the truth of the living word in the Bible, he was concerned to accept new knowledge of its background and the results of critical examination of its content. Something of his stance may be seen in his hymns on Amos and Micah:

> Not in Amos' indignation
> is your final word proclaimed;
> but in him who brings salvation
> to the world your love has claimed:
> Jesus, Saviour,
> friend of sinners he is named.
>
> Still the pride of man defies you,
> falsehood wrongs your Spirit pure:
> still injustice crucifies you,
> still our hate you must endure:
> yet your mercy
> our forgiveness does assure.
>
> (*Rejoice Together* Part 2, 32) see page 21

His hymn inspired by Micah similarly applied the teaching of the Old Testament prophets to the society of his own time. The message is simple but full of force and urgency (conveyed by the short lines):

> What does the Lord require
> for praise and offering?
> What sacrifice desire
> or tribute bid you bring?
> Do justly,
> love mercy;
> walk humbly with your God.
>
> (*Rejoice Together* Part 2, 35) see page 22

Albert was aware that society needed the vision of Micah, and that in the mid-twentieth century that vision was not being heeded. He warned:

Masters of wealth and trade,
  all you for whom men toil,
think not to win God's aid,
  if lies your commerce soil.
    Do justly,
    love mercy;
walk humbly with your God.

(*Rejoice Together* Part 2, 35) see page 22

At the same time as he was repeating the words of the Old Testament prophet, he was very much aware of the changes in our understanding of the world, in our social structures, in science and technology, in theology, in our approach to the Bible, in the life of the Church and in our attitude to its mission. He saw clearly that all these changes had affected the climate of faith and that the hymn writer must respond appropriately if his words are to encourage a living, relevant faith for our time. He was particularly fascinated by new discoveries in astronomy and physics (Grace, his widow, remembered his life-long interest in astronomy and how as a youngster he went to the local library and asked for a book on the stars. He was given a book on film stars). After listening to a BBC Third Programme talk on 'Poetry and Science' in January 1949, he wrote:

Lord of the boundless curves of space
  and time's deep mystery,
to your creative might we trace
  all nature's energy.

Your Spirit gave the living cell
  its hidden, vital force,
the instincts which all life impel
  derive from you, their source.

(*Rejoice Together* Part 2, 19) see page 15

The same reverence in the face of the wonder and mystery of life is found in the hymn:

O Lord of every shining constellation
  that wheels in splendour through the midnight sky,
grant us your Spirit's true illumination
  to read the secrets of your work on high.

His ability to accept and use contemporary images—this was the age of the atom bomb and of atomic power—is clearly seen as the hymn continues:

You, Lord, have made the atom's hidden forces,
  your laws its mighty energies fulfil;
teach us, to whom you give such rich resources,
  in all we use, to serve your holy will.

It would be hard to find the spiritual significance of evolution more engagingly expressed than in the third verse:

O Life, awaking life in cell and tissue,
  from flower to bird, from beast to brain of man,
help us to trace, from birth to final issue,
  the sure unfolding of your age-long plan.

(*Rejoice Together* Part 2, 4) see page 4

xxi

Science and technology now touch our lives at so many points that it is surely right to try to express something of their relationship to religious belief. Indeed, Albert was clear that he was not writing just about science: 'the modern hymn-writer's task is not, of course, merely to crowd his lines with as many aspects of contemporary life as he has room for, but to relate these and the thoughts that they evoke imaginatively and effectively to religious faith.'

Although *Rejoice, O people, in the mounting years* was included in *Congregational Praise* (1951), the other hymns were not known to the compilers. When Albert's first collection, entitled *Rejoice O People* was published in 1950, too late to be considered by the editors, there was, according to Erik Routley, 'much gnashing of teeth about what we had missed.' It was typical of Albert's unassuming nature and his approach to the language of his hymns that in later life he saw the need to revise the texts in *Rejoice O People* to change the 'thou' form to 'you' (the quotations above are taken from the revised versions, printed in Part 2 of his last book, *Rejoice Together*).

Rejoice O People was followed in due course by four other books: *Again I Say Rejoice* (1967), *Rejoice Always* (1971), *Rejoice in God* (1977), and *Rejoice Together* (1982). It is no accident that the title of each collection contains the word 'Rejoice', because the word that runs like a golden thread throughout all his hymns is 'JOY'. He knew as well as any that the Gospel is about good news, so the Christian is to rejoice in God. This characteristic is formulated with delightful simplicity in the hymn *Springs of Joy*

> Joy wings to God our song,
>   for all life holds
>   to stir the heart,
>   to light the mind
> and make the spirit strong.
>
> Joy wings our heart and voice
>   to give ourselves
>   to Christ who died
>   and, risen, lives
> that we may all rejoice.
>
> (*Rejoice in God* 4) see page 62

Joy, as Albert knew well, is not a marketable commodity; it is not like a present from a Christmas tree. Christian joy is something that comes from taking the world seriously with all its pain and problems, but seeing these in the light of the love that came down at Christmas, that suffered on Calvary and that rose again on the first Easter Day. So it is closely related to hope. Albert, while seeing the darker side of human life, saw also the wonder of God's intervention in Jesus Christ. This enabled him to reflect not a facile or syrupy optimism but a deeply rooted faith and hope in God.

As each volume was published, his reputation grew and his hymns became better known. The Anglicans in their *100 Hymns For Today* (1969) included five Bayly hymns: *Lord of all good, our gifts we bring to Thee*; *Lord, save the world*; *O Lord of every shining constellation*; *Praise and thanksgiving*; and the much acclaimed *What does the Lord require*. Its successor, *More Hymns for Today* (1980), included two more, *Lord of the boundless curves of space* and *Lord of the home, your only Son*. In the new Methodist hymn book, *Hymns and Psalms* (1983), the editors chose no less than twelve of his hymns, though they omitted two already familiar through *Hymns and Songs* (1969), *O Lord of every shining constellation* and *Lord, whose love in humble service*, the hymn by which he is best known in the USA. In North America his reputation grew steadily and permission to use his hymns in many of the newer hymn books was increasingly requested. *The Hymnal 1982* contains three of his hymns; the Canadian *Voices United* (1996) two. Not surprisingly, perhaps, the new United Reformed Church hymn book, *Rejoice and Sing* (1991) contains seven; *Common Praise*, the new edition of *Hymns Ancient and Modern* (2000), four.

He also inspired others. Robin Leaver, Professor at Westminster Choir College, Princeton (of which Albert was an Honorary Fellow), recalls hearing Fred Pratt Green protest when credited with being the father of the contemporary English hymn, and say that only one person was worthy of that accolade —Albert Bayly: 'He is the father of us all.' Similarly, Erik Routley wrote of Fred Pratt Green, Fred Kaan and Brian Wren as 'the heirs of Albert Bayly':

> who, a generation older than Kaan and Wren, counts as the first of the
> new wave of experimental hymn writers, making some of the first gestures
> towards a hymnody celebrating the scenes, language and special needs of
> modern urban life. (*Christian Hymns Observed* 1983, p.95)

He was felicitously described by Cyril Taylor, the great writer of hymn tunes and hymn book editor, as 'the last of the old and the first of the new.' It was Taylor who introduced a selection of *The Hymns of Albert Bayly, Pioneer*, at a Come and Sing celebration at Westminster Abbey in 1978, an occasion which gave Albert (who was present) much pleasure: 'It is a great thing to rate one of these hymn-singing sessions all to oneself', said Taylor, 'but if you can have the word "pioneer" after your name, it really puts you among the great ones!'

The task of the hymn writer

ALBERT BAYLY believed that hymns for corporate worship needed to be different from poems expressing a private and individual response to experience. They needed to enable the members of a congregation to express their faith, hope and prayer in language which is meaningful to them. They must, therefore, be simple and clear in expression. In his lecture to the London Branch of the Hymn Society in 1968, Albert quoted from words of tribute to the late President Kennedy after his assassination, 'There is a sense in which only small words are big enough.' He suggested that those words might well be taken to heart by hymn writers, and continued:

> To pour into small words and phrases, without bathos, without cliché
> and with a proper feeling for the dignity of worship and the rhythmic
> quality needed in a hymn; to express thus our human response to God in
> his truth and glory and to interpret our human experience in this light—
> that is surely what the hymn writer must try to do. He must be sensitive
> to the knowledge and modes of life and expression of his time, not in
> order to say just what his contemporaries think and feel, but to express the

response of a man of faith to his experience of the world in which he lives.

He recorded his gratitude to the Revd Hubert Oliver, who encouraged him to write hymns in a modern medium. He responded by writing *Thine is the Kingdom, the power and the glory*. This begins conventionally enough, but then goes on:

Power ever pulsing in atom and heart-beat:
glory of great constellations on high ...

Power of the turbine, of aircraft and radar ...

Thine is the power of a crucified life ...

Come in Thy glory, O Christ, with Thy Kingdom;
visit this world of our sinning and shame.
Claim Thy dominion in workshop and city;
rule all our life by the might of Thy Name.

(*Again I Say Rejoice* 6)

He expressed his pleasure in being able to introduce that hymn to the chief turbine designer of Messrs. Parsons of Tyneside, who was also organist and choirmaster of a Congregational Church in Newcastle-upon-Tyne. In similar mood, Albert rejoiced in the developments in human science and technology that in any way liberated the human spirit. During the Apollo 11 moon mission, he wrote *A Hymn For The Space Age* beginning, 'Great Lord of this vast universe' (*Rejoice Again* 13), in celebration of what he believed to be a great human achievement. At the same time he recognised that it is impossible to write thoughtfully and sensitively about modern developments, such as those in nuclear power, without being concerned with the threat they presented to human well-being and the challenge to human conscience. In a carol written for a competition sponsored by Dagenham Youth Centre, he went straight to the point:

Locked in the atom God has stored a secret might,
Energy unmeasured hidden deep from human sight;
Gift of God for blessing, made by man the tool of fear;
Shall it evermore be so?

(*Again I Say Rejoice* 39) see page 38

The importance of making the right decisions in an age of such power is, he saw, vital. It occurs in one of the hymns from the Old Testament: Nahum's dirge over Nineveh is used as the starting point for a hymn which attempts to bring home our human responsibility for the world in which God has set us:

Must we, who over nature hold
imperial sway,
see all its glories manifold
soon pass away?
Must we, whose planes the skies ascend,
whose cities steel and flame defend,
in universal carnage end
our little day?

'So shall it be, except you turn,
   your proud hearts yield .
Except my law of love you learn,
   Your doom is sealed.'

(*Rejoice Together* Part 2, 36) see page 23

Modern dangers and dilemmas, however, arise not just from new developments in science and technology but also from changes in our relationships with one another. In the early 1950s, for example, race relationships in this country had begun to enter a new phase. In a hymn written for a London Missionary Society Children's Rally, Albert tried to relate the Christian faith to that issue:

Long ago when Jesus
   walked in Galilee,
children found a welcome
   at the Saviour's knee.

Now he gives the children
   born in every land,
dark and fair, a blessing,
   from his loving hand.

Redskin, white or yellow,
   black and brown draw near.
Then, since he receives them
   we too hold them dear.

(*Again I Say Rejoice* 50)

Also changing at this time was the understanding of missionary work. With new developments in the understanding of the Church's mission, the sending countries seeing themselves as receiving countries, and a growing partnership in mission, it was no longer possible to sing with conviction some of the older missionary hymns. A new approach was required by the hymn writer. Yet the dominical command remains: 'Go into all the world'. Albert responded to this theme in response to a request for a hymn for a Roman Catholic Vocations Exhibition:

Christ shall all mankind unite,
   love his design fulfil,
science his truth declare,
   power shall obey his will.
His might to save, his right to claim
This great world's life we now proclaim.

(*Again I Say Rejoice* 23) see page 48

His writing was grounded in the Bible, but it was the Bible interpreted for his age. He discovered a rich source of material in the Hebrew prophets and tried to see the message they held for his own day. Always they were seen in the light of the fulfilment of the Old Testament revelation in Jesus Christ. Conservative he was in some ways, but by no means fundamentalist. He agreed with Erik Routley, who declared 'the real scriptural principle in good hymn writing is the spirit of Scripture rather than its attractive, if sometimes misleading letter'

(*Hymns Today and Tomorrow* 1966, p. 105). Routley saw that with the multiplicity of translations of the Bible, it would become increasingly difficult for hymn writers 'to appear biblical by using direct verbal reminiscences.' Routley argued that if they wished to be scriptural, they must attempt to achieve this by being faithful to the underlying ideas, dogmas and patterns of the Bible. This was always Albert's aim. And without denying the importance of individual salvation, Albert recognised the corporate nature of the salvation to which God calls us in Jesus Christ. Without losing his sense of the value of the individual, he was concerned about God's purpose for society, for the common life, for people and nations. At a time when many were concerned only for personal penitence and individual morality, Albert saw the need for hymns with a wider context:

> Lord, save your world; in bitter need
>   your children lift to you their cry;
> we wait your liberating deed
>   to set us free, lest we should die.
>
> Lord, save your world; we strive in vain
>   to save ourselves without your aid;
> what skill and science slowly gain,
>   is soon to evil ends betrayed.
>
> Then save us now, by Jesus' power,
>   and use the lives your love sets free,
> to bring at last the glorious hour
>   when all will find your liberty.

(*Rejoice Together* Part 2, 14) see page 10

In his lecture given to the London Branch of The Hymn Society, Albert summed up his view of the hymn writer's task with a further quotation from Erik Routley's chapter on 'Images for Today', from *Hymns Today and Tomorrow*: 'It seems clear that the modern hymn writer will serve his age best if his argument is clear and religious and based in the truth declared in Scripture, and clothed in words and images that declare his contact and compassion with the world in which he lives.' (p.105) Albert continued:

> The world in which he lives—yes, indeed that certainly includes the world of space travel, nuclear power, rush hours and all the other modern developments ... But not that world alone. After all, although the lives of many of us are deeply affected by these things, a great part of our experience is with aspects of life and the universe which have inspired poets and hymn writers for centuries. And I believe it is still worthwhile trying to convey the response of the Christian mind and heart to such experiences. Nature in its varied aspects and moods is still the everyday environment of millions of people and eagerly sought by millions more when released from daily tasks ... the home and friendship and Christian fellowship, music and the other arts, life's common joys and sorrows, temptations, tasks and trials, the stages in the Christian life, baptism, profession of faith, Christian marriage and so on. I believe, without striving after that which is startlingly new in form or content, the hymn writer will still be able to give modern man a worthwhile expression for his faith, his aspiration, his penitence, his needs, his spiritual experience and his will to serve and to share the purposes of God.

This takes us into the centre of an individual spirituality, and Albert did not neglect that aspect of the Christian faith. It was this that enabled him to join comfortably and completely the immanence and the transcendence of God. He did not separate the two, but was content to put them side by side as witnesses to different aspects of our experience of God.

> High and lifted up,
> Isaiah saw you, Lord,
> by chanting choirs of Seraphim
> eternally adored.
>
> 'Here, O Lord, am I'
> the answer swiftly came,
> 'Send me to tell your majesty,
> your justice to proclaim.'

(*Rejoice Together* Part 2, 25) see page 16

It is much the same in *The Glory of the Christ*.

> I see his glory in the life
> of saint, apostle, martyr, child.
> The hero spirit's holy strife;
> the tender grace of mercy mild.
>   Each life, a mirror of the Lord,
>   reflects his lineaments adored.
>
> O glory passing human praise;
> in book, in Cross, in life revealed;
> upon his loveliness I gaze,
> and find my soul's diseases healed.
>   Till, by his Spirit's grace restored,
>   I bear the image of my Lord.

(*Rejoice Together* Part 2, 22) see page 28

His writing

ALBERT BAYLY was first and foremost a minister of the Gospel. Maurice Leah knew him in that rôle (he began his ministry at Ryton-on-Tyne while Albert was minister at Monkseaton and his parents were members of Albert's church at Hollingreave, Burnley) and as a hymn writer (he collaborated in writing a tune for *Rejoice, O people, in the mounting years*). Maurice said of him: 'Albert was in every way a truly humble Christian minister. It was not in the churches to which he ministered that he found the recognition that came to him later, as pioneer of modern hymn writing ...' He knew that ministry in the local church is never an easy vocation and the best people are not always those who are greatly lauded. The wonder is that Albert managed to write the greater part of his very considerable output while serving as a Congregational (later URC) minister. But what Albert was as a person came out in his hymns. He had high standards and meticulous care for detail, and he was very precise in getting the metre right.

Commissions or special occasions acted as a stimulus to writing. He wrote to fill gaps, such as the need for new harvest hymns (*Praise and thanksgiving*). Or it might be the induction of a minister, the sight of a blue-tit in summer, a request for a hymn for a particular occasion or special theme, that awoke the muse in Albert. Certainly it would begin with an idea. This he would work on until he had a rough study. He would then consult with Grace; if there were things she was not completely happy about, he would settle down and try again. Before publication he was ready to listen to criticism from musicians, hymn writers and a selected group of friends, because he wanted the very best for those who would sing his hymns.

He did not sit lightly to anything that diminished worship or encouraged a degenerate use of words. He considered Sankey's influence on worship rather a mixed blessing, in that it hindered rather than helped people in appreciating the finer qualities of the church's heritage in hymns. He regarded with rather less than enthusiasm the growth of choruses in worship and was not altogether sure about the contribution of the Twentieth Century Church Light Music Group. In the lecture previously referred to, he declared: 'It would be a pity if the attempt to be "with it" and to make a popular appeal with colloquial phrasing and easy rhythm established a new Sankey tradition which undid any of the good work pioneered by the authors of *Songs of Praise* in raising the general standard of faith in both words and music.'

Albert took seriously Erik Routley's advice to consider a return to the carol in our public praise as a first step to good hymn writing, and produced a number of Christmas carols. Two of these he made reference to in his lecture, 'Hymn Writing for our Times': *I saw a Child of Bethlehem* (*Again I Say Rejoice* 49) and *If Christ were born in Burnley*:

> If Christ were born in Burnley
>   this Christmas night,
>   this Christmas night;
> I know not if the moors would shine
>   with heav'nly light,
>   with heav'nly light.
>   But this I know,
>   my heart would glow,
> and all its inner radiance show,
> if Christ were born in Burnley.
>
> If Christ were born in Burnley.
>   this Christmas day,
>   this Christmas day;
> I know not if the busy throng
>   would bid him stay
>   would bid him stay.
>   But he might rest,
>   my heart's own guest,
> of praise and glory worthiest;
> if Christ were born in Burnley.

(*Rejoice Together* Part 2, 44) see page 11

He always acknowledged the help and encouragement he received from Routley, especially in the provision of tunes (Albert wrote in a great number of different metres). On occasion he would send off as many as six hymn texts, inviting Routley to suggest tunes, after he had gone through various hymn books himself. To many other composers and friends Albert constantly paid tribute. He acknowledged his indebtedness to John Wilson for getting him to alter a word or two of his *Easter Carol* (*Again I Say Rejoice* 57), see page 68, to make it more suitable for Eastertide rather than just Easter Day. But while Albert was always glad to have the comments and criticisms of friends, and was ready to make accommodations where these seemed to be advisable, he was usually firm on things that he wanted to say. He did not like publishers changing the text without consultation. Nor was it appreciated when one church group, without asking permission, added a chorus to one of his children's hymns, *We praise you, O God, for these wonderful days* (*Rejoice Together* Part 1, 12), see page 70. *The Lutheran Book of Worship* (1978) made one or two alterations to the texts which Albert eventually sanctioned, even though he was not very happy about them. More justifiable changes he saw differently. When the compilers were busy preparing *New Church Praise* and Brian Wren suggested a 'rethinking' of his hymn *Lord of the boundless curves of space*, Albert did not turn a hair, even though it meant the abandoning of the last four of his verses and the substitution of three of Wren's to bring in the ideas of Teilhard de Chardin. Both authors had too much respect for each other and their craft to see in the remodelling anything more than the kind of collaboration which is mutually enriching.

In general, Albert would not give way if people wanted to change things he wanted to say without giving adequate reason. More recently there has come to light not only the alteration of a Bayly hymn without permission, but the publication of its text with an ascription to another author. The text, a variant of *Our Father, whose creative love* (*Again I Say Rejoice* 25), see page 54, was submitted to Oxford University Press with request for permission to use the tune St Botolph, which is under their copyright control. It was in this way that it was discovered that an error in authorship had occurred, initially in a Canadian book. This was about to be compounded, with the same inaccurate ascription and even further variations, in an American publication.

Equally controversial for the hymn writer of Albert's day was the tendency to move from the 'thee' and 'thou' to the 'you' and 'your' form of address to God. Albert had a fairly open mind about this, but the older forms came more easily and naturally to him than the new. Like many of his generation, he felt that there was a case for distinguishing the mode of address to God from that which we use to one another. In 1968 he declared:

> Once the novelty has worn off, I doubt if its use will any longer convey any greater feeling of reality or contemporary relevance than the older form. Moreover our present heritage of hymns is almost entirely in that older form and most such hymns could not be recast satisfactorily in the new. It would be a tragedy to abandon this heritage or to date it unnecessarily by writing all new hymns in a different form. However it is possible that the argument for this change will eventually prevail and that we must be prepared to use the two modes of address to God side by side for a long time.

Characteristically, he was prepared to see the other side of the argument, and became more reconciled to the new forms of address. He recast his first book, *Rejoice O People* in the 'you' form and republished the hymns as Part 2 of *Rejoice Together*, more than thirty years after they had first been written.

One of the characteristics of Albert Bayly's writing is that of resolute and splendid simplicity. His style is largely conservative. His language is free from contemporary jargon, and yet it is always fresh and vivid. He was essentially a craftsman who learned his trade with diligence and disciplined effort. Early on he had learned that strictness of form and structure permits a certain liberty and freedom that is dangerous without an underlying discipline. This was true both of his life and his writing. His fastidious choice of word and form was quickly seen if anyone, on taking leave of him, chose to use the informal 'bye-bye'. Albert would reply in almost reproachful fashion, 'Good-bye'. And yet his writing style, though dealing at times with formidable issues, is never heavy or forbidding. As his writing developed, it revealed a lightness of touch, a felicity of image, an imaginative reach and what Stanley Osborne describes as 'a forward thrust'. He had also a breadth of imagination and interest that enabled him to move easily and naturally from tribute to the Apollo Moon Mission (*Rejoice Again* 20), see page 103; from a picture of Christ in a Displaced Persons' Camp (*Again I Say Rejoice* 46), see page 52, to a sonnet, *To a house-martin released from a window* (*Rejoice Again* 16), see page 101.

While the hymn was Albert's favourite vehicle, he did use sonnet form and other forms of writing. In 1953, at the suggestion of the late Dr W.S. Lloyd Webber, Principal of the London College of Music and organist and choirmaster at the Methodist Central Hall, Westminster, Albert wrote the text of the Easter Cantata, *The Divine Compassion*. Lloyd Webber wrote the music. It was sung in the Kingsway Hall, Holborn. Some time later Albert learnt with interest that it was being performed at his old school in Hastings. He was able to write to say that he was an old boy of the school. This cantata was followed by one for Harvest, *Look on the Fields*, and one for Christmas, *Song of Bethlehem*.

Some of his most celebrated sonnets were occasioned by some special event like the unveiling of a plaque on the manse at Thaxted, recording the residence there of Gustav Holst. The sonnet was read at the ceremony by Sir Adrian Boult, who unveiled the plaque:

> Here was great music born: these walls have heard
> New strains spring living from creative thought.
> Here song and symphony took shape, and brought
> A strange new beauty to the hearts they stirred ...

(*Again I Say Rejoice* 81) see page 97

There was also the opening of the new residences at his old college by Her Majesty Queen Elizabeth, the Queen Mother:

> These doors now opened by a royal hand
> shall be a gateway for the King of Kings;
> that young lives, hearing the command he brings,
> shall learn to bear his truth from land to land;
> till from the good seed of the Gospel springs
> a Kingdom's harvest that shall ever stand.

(*Again I Say Rejoice* 77) see page 94

Perhaps most moving of all is this poem written during a period of diminished sight, a thankful outpouring for all that the gift of sight had given him over the years and also a prayer for the inner vision:

I have seen beauty in the hills,
on heather moors and alpine snows,
Orion mounting in the autumn night,
and white sea-horses racing from the shore;
the beauty of a rose, of gulls in flight,
and loveliness of human form and eyes …

When age dims outward sight, give me, O Lord,
that inner vision which can see, within,
the beauty hidden from the outward eye …

Give me love's vision most of all,
to see your greatness humble in a Child;
your glory in a Cross of pain and shame,
your mercy working through life's darkest hours
to bring me to eternal life and joy.
And in the light this inner vision lends,
help me to walk with you in humble love,
until all darkness ends, and I rejoice
to see the glory of your perfect day.

(*Rejoice in God* 25) see page 110

As others saw him

CARYL MICKLEM, the distinguished hymn writer, spoke of Albert's work at the Thanksgiving Service at Christ Church, Chelmsford, in October 1984:

I can't think of a line in his work that is there just for effect—there, just to give people a comfortable feeling, or make them applaud the author's insight or with-it-ness. He wrote, just as he conducted the rest of his ministry, as a servant of the word already given us. He never permitted himself the indulgence of a false stress in his prosody. You never come across a 'tum-te' where it ought to be a 'te-tum' and, if you think you have, it is probably because you're singing the hymn to a tune other than the one Albert first thought of. Musicians liked composing for him because he doesn't let them down.

He spoke of Albert as a true architect, demonstrating his skill not only with his large-scale pieces, such as *Rejoice, O people, in the mounting years*, but also in his more ordinary-size hymns: 'The shape of salvation history, from creation, through patriarchs and prophets, culminating in Christ, leading through to the age of the Spirit and the final fulfilment … is discernible again and again in Albert's hymns. The outlines, miniaturised … but perfect, contracted to a span, but all there.' There is not the slightest air of contrivance or artificiality in Albert's work: 'We feel, don't we, that Albert has not so much made something himself, as grasped the given, and allowed that given to present itself to us, through his craftsmanship, in a manageable and yet memorable form.' Micklem concluded:

Singing or reading his work one is impressed again and again by the youthfulness in the best sense, the youthfulness of Albert's mind. His sense of wonder and delight never turns 'samey' or stale. His sensitivity to the world's pain and need never gets calloused over. And he's never nostalgic. His eye is on the present and on the future, in hope and entreaty to God. He feels the amazement of modern man at the vast emptiness of space and the power-packed density of the atom. His compassion is wide but never strident. His confidence is unwavering but never smug, never facile. Full of realism about our human frailties, he is also full of joy, the authentic joy which comes from God through the Gospel, and which then wings our song back towards God in the praise of the Church.

Brian Wren, another fine contemporary hymn writer, wrote:

His hymn-writing is inseparable from his personality ... He impressed me as a lovable, gentle man, without pretentiousness, truly humble and open to new ideas. I have a poor memory for faces, but his smile stays in my memory. As a hymn writer, he had an ear for the music of the English language. I have read many of his hymns, and never found a sound sequence that was ugly or discordant. This aspect of the hymn-writer's craft is not always appreciated, though it is noticeable if absent. Albert's ear for the sound and rhythm of words is one of my models as I write, and is an outstanding feature of his work. Of the 'hymn explosion' in Britain he was the forerunner. He began writing long before the rest of us, with idioms from an earlier time, but with a range of thought distinctively twentieth-century ... I remember his flexibility, and willingness to take new concerns on board. If he was writing today I'm certain he would be dealing with today's theological issues, not repeating the themes of yesterday.

Fred Pratt Green, in years a contemporary of Albert Bayly, said of him in a tribute in *The Methodist Recorder* in October 1984:

All of us who knew Albert Bayly as a fellow-member of The Hymn Society held him in deep and affectionate regard ... He lived to find himself honoured as the forerunner of the remarkable revival of hymn-writing in the 1960s and 1970s, and to share in it. His reputation as a hymn writer of significance is now recognised throughout the English-speaking world.

He went on to quote Harry Eskew, the American hymnologist: 'Bayly's work, while imaginatively relating the church's worship to the issues of contemporary life, is thoroughly theological and basically conservative in language', adding 'This is true. Albert Bayly was not only aware of the importance for religion of science and technology, he was above all else a most humane man, who did not shrink from the social implications of the gospel he preached.'

Robin Leaver, of Westminster Choir College, Princeton, said of him: 'In terms of relating theology to life in the twentieth century, he was a master craftsman.' After describing *What does the Lord require* as being one of the classic hymns of the twentieth century, he describes it as 'a marvellous text which reflects the rediscovery of Biblical doctrine made in the 1930s and 1940s by many theologians.' He concludes: 'Albert was able to write some very strong texts—picking up contemporary images and using them in a natural way so that you accept the image as self-evident without becoming involved in a "double-take" over its newness.' Citing *O Lord of every shining constellation*, he added 'At that time we were only just coming to terms with "the atom's hidden forces", yet Albert was able to use the phrase in a powerful and telling way, without any pretentious note of novelty.'

Eric Sharpe, a retired Baptist minister, wrote a tribute in the *Baptist Times* in October 1984, in which he described Albert as the doyen of modern hymn writers:

> He was one of the first to see that science and technology and other contemporary influences had opened up areas of experience almost untouched by hymn writers. He had been writing hymns for nearly forty years, and to the end we find the same breadth of thought, linked with simplicity of language, which makes no concessions to the banal and trivial which disfigure so much current writing. Characteristic both of his work and of the man himself is one of the latest hymns he wrote on the theme of Growing:

> > Thanks be to God for all that keeps us growing,
> >   growing in spirit, though the flesh decays:
> > more truth to fill our treasure-house of knowing,
> >   visions of glory moving us to praise.

> (*Rejoice Together* Part 1, 3) see page 70

Conclusion

IN THE preface to *Again I Say Rejoice*, Albert quoted the American author, Don Marquis, who said that 'publishing a volume of verse is like dropping a rose-petal down the Grand Canyon and waiting for the echo.' In his own book, *A Minister Talks To God*, he wrote:

> Your Word shall never be in vain.
> I may have sown a seed
> that will germinate in another mind;
> and your gift to me will grow and flower
> to bear a harvest
> richer than I had ever hoped to see.

There are echoes of Albert's work being heard in many parts of the English-speaking world and he has undoubtedly sown seed that will germinate in many another mind and bear a harvest richer than he in his modest way had ever hoped to see.

Let the last word be that of Fred Pratt Green, *In Memory of Albert F. Bayly*:

> We count you now among the pioneers;
> for you, dear friend, had reached this land before us.
> Before the dawn of our explosive years.

> You staked no claim, issued no manifesto;
> and yet the songs you sang with quiet voice
> pointed the way we knew we had to go.

Perhaps you learned from us, as we from you;
your talent flowered and fruited in old age,
in sharpened language and in rhythms new.

Therefore we come to lay our wreath of words
not on your grave but where a rose is planted,
saying: 'Rejoice—the glory is the Lord's!'

(*The Hymn*, Hymn Society of America, October 1984)

DAVID DALE
1988, revised 2004

The Hymns

A HYMN OF THE WORLD-WIDE CHURCH

Rejoice, O people, in the mounting years
wherein God's mighty purposes unfold.
From age to age his righteous reign appears,
from land to land the love of Christ is told.
   Rejoice, O people, in your glorious Lord,
   lift up your hearts in jubilant accord.

2 Rejoice, O people, in the years of old
when prophets' glowing vision lit the way;
till saint and martyr sped the venture bold,
and eager hearts awoke to greet the day.
   Rejoice in God's glad messengers of peace,
   who bore the Saviour's gospel of release.

3 Rejoice, O people, in the deathless fame
won by the saints whose labours blessed our land;
and those who wrought for love of Jesus' name
with art of builder's and of craftsman's hand.
   Rejoice in him whose Spirit gave the skill
   to work in loveliness his perfect will.

4 Rejoice, O people, in this living hour:
low lies man's pride and human wisdom dies;
but on the Cross God's love reveals his power;
and from his waiting church new hopes arise.
   Rejoice that, while the sin of man divides,
   one Christian fellowship of love abides.

5 Rejoice, O people, in the days to be,
when o'er the strife of nations sounding clear,
shall ring love's gracious song of victory,
to east and west his kingdom bringing near.
   Rejoice, rejoice, his church on earth is one,
   and binds the ransomed nations 'neath the sun.

6 Rejoice, O people, in that final day
when all the travail of creation ends;
Christ now attains his universal sway,
o'er heaven and earth his royal Word extends:
   that Word proclaimed where saints and martyrs trod,
   the glorious gospel of the blessèd God.

1945

Tunes NORTHUMBRIA   REJOICE, O PEOPLE

*This, my first hymn, was written in its original form for the Triple Jubilee of the
London Missionary Society in 1945, and set to a tune by the Revd Eric Shave. It
was revised for general use at the request of* The BBC Hymn Book *Committee,
and adopted, with a tune 'Northumbria' by Dr W.K. Stanton. It was afterwards
accepted by the Committee preparing* Congregational Praise *and set to a tune
'Rejoice, O People' by Dr Eric Thiman*

THE KINGDOM OF GOD

Lord, your kingdom bring triumphant,
   give this world your liberty,
may your Spirit's strong compulsion
   rule our tides of energy:

2 Where the vessel cleaves the ocean,
   or the airman flies his plane,
where the miner toils in darkness,
   and the farmer sows the grain.

3 Consecrate your people's labour
   at the airfield, mill and port;
with the gladness of your presence
   bless our homes and grace our sport.

4 Let your mercy and your wisdom
   rule our courts and parliament,
and to soldier, sage and scholar
   may your light and truth be sent.

5 By the pioneer's endeavour,
   by the word of printed page,
by the martyr's dying witness,
   and your saints in every age:

6 By the living voice of preacher,
   by the skill of surgeon's hand,
by the far borne broadcast tidings
   speaking peace from land to land:

7 Lord, your kingdom bring triumphant,
   visit us this living hour,
let your toiling, sinning children
   see your kingdom come in power.

1945

Tunes STUTTGART   LAUS DEO

SHIPS OF THE CHURCH

Lord of the restless ocean,
   whose Son on Galilee
above the storm's commotion
   stood master of the sea;
your name for ever living
   with joyful hearts we greet,
and hail with glad thanksgiving
   the vessels of your fleet.

2 Lord God, whose vast creation
   is heaven's arching dome,
your earthly habitation
   a craftsman's humble home;
for all your Spirit dowers
   accept our praises meet,
whose grace with skill empowers
   the builders of your fleet.

3 O ruler strong, ordaining,
    your word a shining sword,
from Calvary once reigning,
    our captain and our Lord:
our loyalty confessing,
    we fall before your feet,
and join our songs of blessing
    with seamen of your fleet.

4 O Lord, for ever calling
    to ventures new and bold,
with visions still enthralling
    your servants as of old:
O speed our high endeavour,
    we humbly you entreat,
and send us now and ever
    the spirit of your fleet.

1945

Tunes AURELIA LLANGLOFFAN

This hymn was written in 1945 for the Celebration 'God's Man', commemorating Captain James Wilson of the 'Duff', published by the London Missionary Society

GOD'S AGE-LONG PLAN

O Lord of every shining constellation
    that wheels in splendour through the midnight sky,
grant us your Spirit's true illumination
    to read the secrets of your work on high.

2 You, Lord, have made the atom's hidden forces,
    your laws its mighty energies fulfil;
teach us, to whom you give such rich resources,
    in all we use, to serve your holy will.

3 O Life, awaking life in cell and tissue,
    from flower to bird, from beast to brain of man
help us to trace, from birth to final issue,
    the sure unfolding of your age-long plan.

4 You, Lord, have stamped your image on your creatures,
    and, though they mar that image, love them still;
lift up our eyes to Christ, that in his features
    we may discern the beauty of your will.

5 Great Lord of nature, shaping and renewing,
    you made us more than nature's sons to be;
you help us tread, with grace our souls enduing,
    the road to life and immortality.

1945

Tunes RERUM CREATOR   STRENGTH AND STAY   STONOR
      HOLLINGREAVE (*M. Leah*)

CREATIVE JOY

Builder of the starry frame,
  in your handiwork rejoicing,
worship we your glorious Name,
  heartily your praises voicing.

2 For your creatures you have planned
    taste of your divine enjoyment;
  we, in arts of mind or hand
    share your Spirit's high employment.

3 Craftsman, writer, artist, sage,
    serve your purpose and your pleasure;
  singer's voice and poet's page
    echo your melodious measure.

4 Yet a joy more precious still
    we, whom you created, owe you,
  when our heart obeys your will
    we may truly come to know you.

5 When your grace forms Christ in man,
    crowning thus your whole creation,
  we, in your redemptive plan,
    share the joy of your salvation.

6 Heartily we then rejoice,
    music to your glory making,
  grateful soul and thankful voice
    in one joyous song awaking.

1945

Tune JORDANIS ORAS PRÆVIA

A CHILDREN'S HYMN OF THE CHURCH

A glorious company we sing,
  the Master and his men:
he sent them forth to tell his love
  by voice and hand and pen.
Then with his Spirit's mighty flame
  he made their hearts to glow,
and bade them on a troubled world
  his grace and power bestow.

5

2   A faithful company we sing,
    the steadfast martyr band:
against the rage of ruler proud
    they boldly made their stand:
and still when men defy Christ's name,
    the cross is raised on high,
and for his sake his hosts go forth
    to battle and to die.

3   A daring company we sing,
    who bore by land and sea
the tidings of their Saviour's love,
    his cross and victory.
Till east and west and north and south
    rejoice in glad accord,
and all the world's great peoples hail
    the kingdom of the Lord.

4   A company of love we sing,
    whom Jesus called to save
all sick and blind and hungry folk,
    the outcast and the slave:
and now when life of man or child
    is hurt by sin and pain,
he calls for eager willing hands
    to share his love again.

5   O we would join this company
    of Jesus and his friends;
this church which now in every land
    the reign of Christ extends:
and may that Spirit which of old
    his servants did inspire
with love and joy and faith and power
    set all our hearts afire.

1946

Tunes   DAVID   ELLACOMBE

*This hymn was written for a Sunday School Anniversary
celebration, 'In the power of the Spirit', given at Morpeth
Congregational Church in July 1946. It was published in*
The Sunday School Chronicle *on September 19th 1946*

THE SPIRIT OF GOD

Fire of God, undying flame,
Spirit who in splendour came,
let your heat my soul refine,
   till it glows with love divine.

2 Breath of God that swept in power
   in the Pentecostal hour;
holy breath, be now in me
   source of vital energy.

3 Strength of God, your might within,
   conquers sorrow, pain and sin;
fortify from evil art
   all the gateways of my heart.

4 Truth of God your piercing rays
   penetrate my secret ways,
may the light that shames my sin
   guide me holier paths to win.

5 Love of God, your grace profound
   knows not either age or bound;
come, my heart's own guest to be,
   dwell for evermore in me

April 1947

Tunes VIENNA SAVANNAH

THE WORD OF GOD

Your Word, O God, awoke the uncreated;
   brought form from chaos, out of darkness, light:
till life, by silent ages long awaited,
   displayed its growing beauty in your sight.
In field and forest, ocean, air and river,
   your eyes beheld your creatures very good;
and quickened by your breath, Almighty Giver;
   your human image in your presence stood.

2 Your Word, O God, awoke prophetic voices
   on Carmel's height, and Judah's rocky hills;
the great Isaiah's ardent soul rejoices,
   and Jeremiah's tortured bosom thrills.
To sage and psalmist comes your inspiration,
   in song sublime and wisdom's subtle page;
and in the law and records of a nation,
   your Word, O God, speaks on from age to age.

3 Your Word, O God, took flesh for our salvation,
   and we beheld his glory, truth and grace;
he brings the Gospel of our liberation,
   the tidings of your mercy light his face.
In healing deeds of love and holy story
   we hear the music of your gracious Name;
still more, his Cross and resurrection glory
   the sovereign triumphs of your love proclaim.

7

4 Now speak again your Word unto the nations,
    in all the fulness of your Spirit's power;
and as your voice woke former generations,
    declare your purpose for this present hour.
O speak to smite, to cleanse and to renew us,
    your church awaits the judgment of your sword;
until with power your Spirit shall endue us
    to give the world the Gospel of our Lord.

April 1947

Tune LONDONDERRY AIR

MANSFIELD CHAPEL
Commemoration and Valediction
'Deus locutus est nobis in filio'

Your voice, O Lord, through growing years
    has spoken in these sacred walls;
each passing generation hears
    your summons which to service calls.
O voice of God, speak to us still,
    and send us forth to do your will.

2 From sculptured niche and storied pane
    a host of witnesses look down;
while younger athletes strive to gain
    the prize of truth's immortal crown.
O make us strong to run our race,
    and lift our eyes to Jesus' face.

3 You gave us wisdom's precious lore,
    true friends whose love has been our wealth;
and from your mercy's boundless store,
    we draw forgiveness, courage, health.
May we this heritage employ,
    that men may know your love and joy.

4 That voice which our forefathers heard
    from prophet's tongue in diverse ways,
by your own Son, the living Word,
    has spoken in these latter days.
Now we would hear your Spirit's call,
    and in your service offer all.

June 1947

Tunes REST   FARMBOROUGH

Inspired by the Mansfield College, Oxford, Old Men's meetings.
Printed in the College magazine in August 1947

PRAYER FOR DELIVERANCE

Your love, O God, has all mankind created,
    and led your people to this present hour:
in Christ we see love's glory consummated;
    your Spirit manifests his living power.

2 We bring you, Lord, in fervent intercession,
        the children of your world-wide family:
    with contrite hearts we offer our confession,
        for we have sinned against your charity.

3 From out the darkness of our hope's frustration;
        from all the broken idols of our pride;
    we turn to seek your truth's illumination;
        and find your mercy waiting at our side.

4 In pity look upon your children's striving
        for life and freedom, peace and brotherhood;
    till at the fulness of your truth arriving,
        we find in Christ the crown of every good.

5 Inspire your church, mid earth's discordant voices,
        to preach the gospel of her Lord above;
    until the tired, warring world rejoices
        to hear the mighty harmonies of love.

6 Until the tidings earth has long awaited,
        from north to south, from east to west shall ring;
    and all mankind, by Jesus liberated,
        proclaims in jubilation, Christ is King!

May 1947

Tunes INTERCESSOR CHARTERHOUSE

Suggested by the Triple Jubilee of the Church Missionary Society

INVOCATION

Lord God, whose Spirit lit the flame
    that burned within Isaiah's soul;
when, bowed before your face in shame
    his lips were purged with living coal;
Lord, touch our hearts with cleansing fire,
set us ablaze with pure desire.

2 Lord God, who in that blackest hour,
        when Christ entombed in darkness lay;
    did manifest your living power
        at dawn of resurrection day;
    shed on our world of death and strife
    your Spirit's gift of risen life.

3 Lord God, whose mighty breath inspired
    the waiting apostolic band;
by whom the heart of Paul was fired
    to tell of Christ from land to land;
grant us your vital energy
your Spirit's witnesses to be.

4 Now in this hour when faith burns low,
    and shattered lies our proudest plan,
when ancient evils rankly grow,
    and fears possess the heart of man;
Lord God of fire and life and light,
revive us with your Spirit's might.

October 1947

Tunes DURA   FALKLAND

THE WORLD'S NEED

L ord, save your world; in bitter need
  your children lift to you their cry;
we wait your liberating deed
    to set us free, lest we should die.

2 Lord, save your world; our souls are bound
    in iron chains of fear and pride;
high walls of ignorance around
    our faces from each other hide.

3 Lord, save your world; we strive in vain
    to save ourselves without your aid;
what skill and science slowly gain
    is soon to evil ends betrayed.

4 Lord, save your world; but you have sent
    the Saviour whom we sorely need;
for us his tears and blood were spent,
    that from our bonds we might be freed.

5 Then save us now, by Jesus' power,
    and use the lives your love sets free,
to bring at last the glorious hour
    when all will find your liberty.

November 1947

Tunes MAINZER   UFFINGHAM

THE SOUL'S STAR

My soul, your only star
    shines high above;
adore him from afar,
    your Lord of love.

2 Adore him from afar;
       most holy he;
   no sin and error mar
       his purity.

3 Yet his light shines within
       your secret heart;
   the darkness of your sin
       he bids depart.

4 To watch you and to guide
       he lights your way;
   lest from the truth aside
       your footsteps stray.

5 Then all my soul adore
       your star divine;
   to him for evermore
       your heart incline.

6 To him for evermore
       your worship pay;
   and all love's richest store
       in tribute lay.

November 1947

Tune EDMUNDS WALK

The first line of this hymn came to me in a dream

A CHRISTMAS CAROL

If Christ were born in Burnley
       this Christmas night,
       this Christmas night;
I know not if the moors would shine
       with heav'nly light,
       with heav'nly light.
       But this I know,
       my heart would glow,
and all its inner radiance show,
       if Christ were born in Burnley.

2   If Christ were born in Burnley
       this Christmas-tide,
       this Christmas-tide;
I know not if with treasures rare
       the wise would ride,
       the wise would ride.
       But I would bring
       my offering,
to kneel and worship hastening;
       if Christ were born in Burnley.

11

3   If Christ were born in Burnley
        this Christmas day,
        this Christmas day;
  I know not if the busy throng
        would bid him stay,
        would bid him stay.
        But he might rest,
        my heart's own guest,
  of praise and glory worthiest;
        if Christ were born in Burnley.

1947

Tune FAIRHOLME ROAD (*M. Leah*)

*The fine moors around Burnley helped to inspire this carol.
Other place names may be used, or 'in my town' or 'where I live' substituted.
'Fields' may be read for 'moors'*

A HYMN FOR HOMEMAKERS

Lord of the home, your only Son
  received a mother's tender love;
and from an earthly father won
  his vision of your home above.

2 Help us, O Lord, our homes to make
    your Holy Spirit's dwelling place;
  our hands and hearts' devotion take
    to be the servants of your grace.

3 Pray we that all who with us dwell,
    your love and joy and peace may know;
  and while our lips your praises tell,
    may faithful lives your glory show.

4 Teach us to keep our homes so fair,
    that were our Lord a child once more,
  he might be glad our hearth to share,
    and find a welcome at our door.

5 Lord, may your Spirit sanctify
    each household duty we fulfil;
  may we our Master glorify
    in glad obedience to your will.

1947

Tunes WESTFIELDS (*M.Leah*) WARRINGTON ILLSLEY

*Written in 1947 for the Young Wives' Fellowship, Hollingreave
Congregational Church, Burnley, at the request of my wife*

THE JOY OF LIFE

O joy of life, when full and strong,
the tide of youth flows in the blood;
how free and jubilant its song,
the music of its brimming flood.

2 O joy of life, a deeper strain
sounds clearer with advancing years;
above the harsher chords of pain,
its triumph echoes in our ears.

3 O joy of life, when calmly flows
time's river to the larger sea;
and nobly in the distance grows
the music of eternity.

4 O joy of life, enduring joy,
when Christ within the heart abides;
no ill their gladness can destroy
whose hope secure in God confides,

February 1948

Tunes WINCHESTER NEW BROCKHAM

This hymn was suggested to me by a visit to 'Lilac Time'

A HYMN FOR AMSTERDAM

With jubilant united strain,
one song we sing.
From mountain, isle and peopled plain,
our praise we bring.
We bear the nations' treasure store,
their glory and their honour pour,
with grateful offering adore
our God and King.

2 We greet the day which prophet eyes
desired to see:
when round the world your sons arise,
whom Christ made free.
From every nation, tongue and race,
we tell the story of your grace;
and lift our eyes to Jesus' face,
one family.

3 With humble hearts we wait to hear
    your Spirit's call.
Your judgment sounds upon our ear;
    in shame we fall.
Then cleansed, forgiven and restored,
we rise to serve our living Lord,
and with your Holy Spirit's sword
    to conquer all.

4 One God we know, one Faith we teach,
    one Lord proclaim,
one Saviour to the nations preach,
    for aye the same.
Though kingdoms rise and change and end,
your reign, O Christ, shall still extend;
and every knee in worship bend,
    at your great Name.

August 1948

Tune AMSTERDAM HYMN (*Eric Shave*)

*I wrote this just before attending the Amsterdam Assembly
of the World Council of Churches. It was published in*
The Christian World. *The tune 'Amsterdam Hymn' was
composed for it by the Revd. Eric Shave* MA, *of Streatham
Congregational Church*

IN GRATEFUL TRIBUTE TO ISAAC WATTS

Your glory filled the place,
    when temple choirs of old,
the story of your grace,
in joyous anthems told.
    Our voice we raise
    that glory still
    your house may fill
    when we bring praise.

2 Your glory moved the heart
    of sacred bard to sing,
with consecrated art,
his praise to heaven's King.
    With grateful voice
    we lift again
    the holy strain;
    and all rejoice.

3 Your glory still appears
    in every age the same,
when singers, poets, seers
make music to your Name.
    Lord, haste the hour
    when all will raise
    one hymn of praise,
    and own your power.

4 Your perfect glory shone
    through him in whom we heard
the voice of your own Son,
the music of your Word.
    Then let us sing
    in full accord:
    and to our Lord
    all honour bring.

November 1948

Tunes DARWALL'S 148TH HAREWOOD

Inspired by the Isaac Watts bi-centenary

CREATOR AND REDEEMER

L ord of the boundless curves of space
and time's deep mystery,
to your creative might we trace
all nature's energy.

2 Your mind conceived the galaxy,
each atom's secret planned,
and every age of history
your purpose, Lord, has spanned.

3 Your Spirit gave the living cell
its hidden, vital force;
the instincts which all life impel
derive from you, their source.

4 Yours is the image stamped on man,
though marred by man's own sin;
and yours the liberating plan
again his soul to win.

5 Science explores your reason's ways,
and faith can more impart:
for in the face of Christ our gaze
looks deep within your heart.

6 Christ is your wisdom's perfect word,
your mercy's crowning deed:
in him the sons of earth have heard
your strong compassion plead.

7 Give us to know your truth, but more,
the strength to do your will;
until the love our souls adore
shall all our being fill.

January 1949

Tunes SAN ROCCO   SALZBURG   CAITHNESS

*Suggested by a BBC Third Programme talk on
poetry and science by J. Isaacs on January 17th 1949*

A Series of Hymns on the Hebrew Prophets

ISAIAH

High and lifted up,
   Isaiah saw you, Lord,
by chanting choirs of Seraphim
   eternally adored.

2 'Woe is me' he cried,
 'To see his holy face;
a man of unclean lips am I
 and born of unclean race.'

3 Purged with living flame,
 your voice Isaiah heard;
'Whom shall I send, and who will go
 to speak my holy word?'

4 'Here, O Lord, am I'
 the answer swiftly came,
'Send me to tell your majesty,
 your justice to proclaim.'

5 High and lifted up
 you are, but now we trace
in Christ uplifted on the Cross
 the mercy in your face.

6 Here, O Lord, are we;
 our hearts and lips prepare,
and send us into all the world,
 your truth and love to share.

March 1948

Tune COLEMAN'S HATCH (*Erik Routley*)

THE PROPHET OF THE RETURN

O joyful hope, in weary hearts awaking:
O blessed voice of pardon and release:
tidings of grace for souls oppressed and aching;
telling of liberation, life and peace.
    'Comfort ye my people, saith your God:
    my people, comfort ye'.

2 Long was the night of exiled Israel's sorrow;
bitter the hours of suffering and fear:
till on her darkness dawned the light of morrow;
when prophet lips proclaimed redemption near.
    'Comfort ye my people, saith your God:
    my people, comfort ye.'

3 Now for mankind a brighter dawn has broken;
bidding the gloom of sin and death be gone.
God's voice of love his perfect Word has spoken;
Jesus the light of all the world is born.
    'Comfort ye my people, saith your God:
    my people, comfort ye.'

4 Lift up your voices then, in exultation;
tell every land the tidings you have heard:
Jesus proclaims his people's liberation;
speaks in the Cross his Father's saving Word.
    'Comfort ye my people, saith your God;
    my people, comfort ye.'

December 1948

Tune COMFORT YE

JEREMIAH

Your Spirit, Lord, in years of old
made timid Jeremiah strong;
inspired his lips, and made him bold
to smite the tyranny of wrong.
    Give us his courage, Lord, that we
    your faithful witnesses may be.

2 Your Spirit gave him strength to bear
the lies and malice of his foes;
the stab of pain, the strain of care,
the agony of Judah's woes.
    Help us his fortitude to win,
    beneath the hot assaults of sin.

3 Your flaming word within him burned,
   and fired his tongue your truth to tell;
   though men its warning rudely spurned,
   like hammer on the rock it fell.
     Inspired by your word's energy,
     may all we utter fearless be.

4 When Judah's life in ruin lay,
   your sentence on her broken bond;
   he pierced the gloom of judgment day,
   and saw the Covenant beyond.
     Lord, teach us in the darkest hour
     to trust your love's unfailing power.

5 O life of loneliness and pain;
   yet from that pain what hope was born!
   for Jesus Christ has made again
   the Covenant by Judah torn.
     Now all mankind, from sin restored,
     may share your love, and know you Lord.

March 1948

Tunes   PATER OMNIUM   VATER UNSER (OLD 112TH)

EZEKIEL

Lord, your Spirit's quick'ning breath
roused the silent ranks of death;
when Ezekiel's prophet tones
woke the dry and lifeless bones.
  Let our souls like them be stirred
  by your life-inspiring word.

2 Amber beams of radiant light
   marked your chariot's onward flight:
   winged and wheeled, the fiery car
   bore your glory from afar.
     Lord, upon our watching eyes,
     let your majesty arise.

3 When the prophet's pleading failed,
   still your mighty love prevailed:
   you have promised to your own
   hearts of flesh for hearts of stone.
     Gracious Father, when we sin,
     do your saving work within.

4 Life and light and love we see
   in your perfect Trinity:
   all in fullest glory shone
   in the face of Christ your Son.
     Let your glory on us shine,
     work in us your love's design.

November 1948

Tunes   HEATHLANDS   RATISBON

DANIEL

L ord of the brave in every age;
who, fearing neither sword nor flame,
withstood the cruel tyrant's rage;
Jehovah! we adore your Name.
   'No other gods we serve,
   no other lordship own;
from your commands we will not swerve,
   but worship you alone.'

2 Proudly the Babylonian king
before his image bids men fall;
but three will no submission bring;
upon your Name alone they call.
   'No other gods we serve,
   no other lordship own;
from your commands we will not swerve,
   but worship you alone.'

3 Brief is the tyrant's evil hour;
no furnace flame nor lion's den
can overcome your Spirit's power,
or break the will of faithful men.
   'No other gods we serve,
   no other lordship own;
from your commands we will not swerve,
   but worship you alone.'

4 Give us the eyes of faith to see
like Daniel, your eternal plan
fulfilled, when all authority
is given to the Son of Man.
   'No other gods we serve,
   no other lordship own;
from your commands we will not swerve,
   but worship you alone.'

5 Ancient of days, enthroned above
the fallen images of pride;
your everlasting reign of love
shall, over all, through Christ, abide.
   'No other gods we serve,
   no other lordship own;
from your commands we will not swerve,
   but worship you alone.'

December 1948

HOSEA

O faithful love, enduring still,
   though in your very shrine betrayed;
no mockery or falsehood swayed
the saving purpose of your will.

2 Your covenant in days of old,
   to Abraham and Moses sworn;
   by Israel's wayward heart was torn;
   her loyalty to idols sold.

3 Until, prophetic of the Cross,
   Hosea your agony revealed;
   the love which man's backsliding healed
   by Christ our Saviour's bitter loss.

4 O love divine, in Christ we find
   the fulness of your sacrifice;
   the whole immeasurable price
   you gave to win back lost mankind.

5 Lord, we are children you have taught
   to walk, by love's own harness led;
   and when in wilfulness we fled,
   your grace our erring footsteps sought.

6 When we, your own beloved, forswore
   for other gods our sacred tryst;
   your love upon the Cross of Christ
   the shame of our betrayal bore.

7 O faithful love, to you we turn,
   our heart's true home again to find.
   That love our wayward souls shall bind,
   no more your sacrifice to spurn.

December 1947

Tunes BRESLAU   WHITEHALL

JOEL

Day of the Lord, how shall we know your coming?
  how shall we see your fateful dawn appear?
angry with fire and heaven's thunder drumming?
  dark with the doom of judgment drawing near?

2 So once the prophet Joel saw in vision
  locust and famine sweeping o'er the land,
multitudes massing for a great decision,
  saw, and proclaimed Jehovah's day at hand.

3 Then, with an eye beyond disaster ranging,
  faith saw the Spirit on mankind outpoured:
saw all the land from dearth to beauty changing
  under the living impulse of the Lord.

4 Old men dream dreams when God brings his salvation:
  young men see visions of his reign to be:
handmaids receive his heav'nly inspiration:
  servants his Spirit's breath of liberty.

5 Day of the Spirit, we have seen your glory
  shining from hearts ablaze with holy flame:
kindling the lips that told the Gospel story:
  glowing in lives that bore the Saviour's Name.

6 Still we await the day of consummation;
  God's fateful day of judgment on mankind:
when at his throne shall men of every nation
  his final verdict on their actions find.

7 Christ will be judge, and deeds his love has gendered,
  shall in that hour alone avail for plea:
'As to my humbler brothers you have rendered,
  so, men and women, you have done to me.'

August 1949

Tunes ST OSYTH   LOMBARD STREET

AMOS

From the hills in wrath descending,
  came Tekoa's shepherd seer;
Israel's fatal slumber rending
  with the cry, 'Your doom is near.'
    God in judgment,
  swift in judgment shall appear.

2 Sacrifice in vain you offer,
  vainly tune your solemn lays;
purer hearts I bid you proffer;
  honest deeds and nobler ways.
    Bring God justice;
  righteous lives his Name shall praise.

3 Lord, we know our own transgression,
    on our sins your judgment falls;
hear, when making our confession,
    each upon your mercy calls;
      for that mercy
    all our deepest need forestalls.

4 Not in Amos' indignation
    is your final word proclaimed;
but in him who brings salvation
    to the world your love has claimed:
      Jesus, Saviour,
    friend of sinners he is named.

5 Still the pride of man defies you,
    falsehood wrongs your Spirit pure:
still injustice crucifies you,
    still our hate you must endure:
      yet your mercy
    our forgiveness does assure.

6 Still we hear your word in thunder,
    but the thunder of love's might.
Now we see in grateful wonder,
    mercy dawn on judgment's night.
      Love triumphant
    breaks in glory on our sight.

December 1947

Tunes ORIEL   ST THOMAS

MICAH

What does the Lord require
    for praise and offering?
What sacrifice desire
    or tribute bid you bring?
      Do justly,
      love mercy;
walk humbly with your God.

2 Rulers of men, give ear!
    Should you not justice know?
Will God your pleading hear,
    while crime and cruelty grow?
      Do justly,
      love mercy;
walk humbly with your God.

3 Masters of wealth and trade.
    all you for whom men toil,
think not to win God's aid,
    if lies your commerce soil.
      Do justly,
      love mercy;
walk humbly with your God.

4 Still down the ages ring
    the prophet's stern commands.
To merchant, worker, king,
    he brings God's high demands.
      Do justly,
      love mercy;
walk humbly with your God.

5 How shall our life fulfil
    God's law so hard and high?
Let Christ endue our will
    with grace to fortify.
      Then justly,
      in mercy;
we'll humbly walk with God.

January 1949

Tune SHARPTHORNE

She was a city proudly strong:
now low she lies.
Her glory, built on tyrant wrong
all broken, dies.
Her foemen's chariots throng the street;
her soldiers flee in wild defeat;
devouring flames her doom complete,
no more to rise.

2 Like Nineveh, man's empires fall;
their splendours wane.
The flashing steel, the stubborn wall,
defend in vain.
The realm that rests on force her trust
will surely crumble into dust;
her might decay, her weapons rust,
no stones remain.

3 Must we, who over nature hold
imperial sway,
see all its glories manifold
soon pass away?
Must we, whose planes the skies ascend,
whose cities steel and flame defend,
in universal carnage end
our little day?

4 'So shall it be, except you turn,
your proud hearts yield.
Except my law of love you learn,
your doom is sealed.'
Then, Lord, forgive our bitter sin;
destroy the pride that lurks within;
your love's dominion o'er us win,
and ever wield.

December 1949

Tune GRAVETYE (*Erik Routley*)

HAGGAI

In ruin lay Jehovah's sacred shrine,
where once his people praised the Name divine:
but now the citizens passed on their way,
all careless of her fate, content to say
   'It is not time to build.'

2 Then Haggai's heart with holy zeal was stirred
   to rouse his people with God's living word.
   'You dwell in comfort, while this house lies waste.
   Leave selfish pleasures; God is calling—haste!
      Now is the time to build!'

3 So Judah's governor and priest arose;
   while all the citizens forsook repose.
   They toiled the fallen temple walls to raise,
   Jehovah's house of sacrifice and praise.
      For it was time to build.

4 Still down the ages Zion's prophet calls;
   when fallen lie the holy temple walls
   our fathers built for glory of God's name;
   now left in ruin, to his people's shame.
      'Rise up, 'tis time to build.'

5 Rebuild the walls! Not only walls of stone;
   but walls that to the spirit's eyes are known;
   the sacred walls of truth and trust and love,
   of fabric God has wrought in realms above;
      wherewith we may rebuild.

6 Arise and build! We answer, Lord, your word:
   our body, mind and soul for labour gird.
   To you all glory! Ours the workers' joy,
   who in your service every power employ.
      We rise, O Lord, to build!

June 1949

ZECHARIAH

Rejoice! O daughter of Jerusalem
your king is coming, and salvation brings.
No tyrant, captive peoples to condemn;
   but Prince of Peace, most merciful of kings.

2 War's bow and chariot he shall destroy;
      and peace bestow on every troubled land.
   The child shall happy hours in play employ,
      the aged safely rest with staff in hand.

24

3 The King has come! In peaceful state he rode
   up Zion's hill, to claim his royal throne.
   But when he entered his beloved abode,
   his citizens refused their Lord to own.

4 For throne they made a cross; his crown was thorn;
   his mocking foes a purple robe did bring;
   by lash and nail his flesh was cruelly torn;
   his very friends denied, betrayed, their King.

5 Yet still he reigns: in triumph from the grave
   he rose to rule his Church, a living Lord.
   In every age he comes anew to save,
   and in our need his precious aid afford.

6 Rejoice, O people! let each heart prepare
   to greet the King who ends all sin and strife.
   Proclaim him Lord; and publish everywhere
   his Name, the Prince of Peace and Love of Life.

April 1949

Tunes TOULON   JULIUS

MALACHI

See! the Lord, in fire appearing,
comes his house to purify.
Levi's Sons, his judgment hearing,
   at his feet repentant lie.
      God all holy,
   with consuming flame is nigh.

2 Like refiner's fire, his burning
      smelts the silver from the ore:
   Israel's sullied off'rings turning
      into precious gifts which pour,
         overflowing;
      from love's consecrated store.

3 Who shall stand at his appearing?
      Who abide his judgment day?
   He alone who his Name fearing
      may enjoy his healing ray;
         when like stubble,
      pride consumed shall pass away.

4 Heralded by prophet voices,
      comes Jehovah's promised hour:
   every faithful heart rejoices;
      God will manifest his power:
         by his Spirit,
      evil utterly devour.

5 Christ is come! God's judgment bringing;
      fire of truth our souls to try.
   Holy fire upon us flinging,
      fire to save and purify:
         fire to fit us
      for immortal life on high.

November 1949

Tunes ORIEL   REGENT SQUARE

I saw a city come from God above,
of beauty pure and rare;
a bride adorned for Christ her husband's love,
in garments rich and fair.

2 The nations bring their glory to her gates;
earth's kings in homage bend.
the expectation of the ages waits
to win in her its end.

3 Beside the clamorous and crowded street,
I walk her quiet ways:
her citizens from every land I meet,
and hear their songs of praise.

4 I see her beauty in the eager eyes
of consecrated youth;
and mirrored in the features of the wise
behold her heav'nly truth.

5 The worker's toil, the dying martyr's pain,
the pangs of motherhood,
all human travail, here at last attain
through Christ their destined good.

6 O city beautiful, thy God shall be
my God, thy people mine;
and I would dwell, beloved home, in thee,
now and for ever thine.

September 1948

Tune LUX VERA

PRAISE IN UNITY

L ord of the nations, living Lord,
Father of earth's great family;
your children everywhere accord
the praise of hearts in unity.
Thanksgiving, worship, love we bring,
your greatness and your glory sing.

2 Lord of the ages, by whose will
kingdoms arise, endure and fall;
your everlasting reign shall still
remain triumphant over all.
Thanksgiving, worship, love, we bring,
your greatness and your glory sing.

3 Father, your grace in Christ your Son
   binds all the races of mankind.
   Around his cross we meet as one,
   and in his Name communion find.
       Thanksgiving, worship, love, we bring,
       your greatness and your glory sing.

4 Spirit of truth, and life, and love,
   kindle us all with holy flame:
   till your whole church, on earth, above,
   declares the grace of Jesus' Name.
       Thanksgiving, worship, love, we bring,
       your greatness and your glory sing.

April 1949

Tunes PATER OMNIUM   DAVID'S HARP

*Written for the Pageant 'God's Building' commemorating
the story of the South India Church, published by the L.M.S.*

EASTER HYMN

Life eternal, life victorious,
from the tomb arising glorious;
love undying, might unfailing;
over sin and death prevailing;
   risen Lord, we hail you!

2 From the bitterness of sorrow,
   fear that dreads to face the morrow,
   from despair and self-delusion,
   from a faithless heart's confusion,
      risen Jesus, save us!

3 Sinless victor in temptation,
   pioneer of our salvation,
   when satanic forces rend us,
   by your holy might defend us,
      risen Lord, we need you!

4 King, to God's right hand ascending;
   love, in mercy on us bending;
   bread, who for our sakes was broken;
   word of life, to sinners spoken;
      risen Christ, accept us!

5 Voices, hearts, we lift in union
   with your saints in one communion;
   all your church, your love confessing,
   bringing honour, glory, blessing;
      risen Lord, for ever!

April 1949

Tune SAINTHILL   (*Erik Routley*)

THE GLORY OF THE CHRIST

I see the glory of the Christ
in gospel writers' holy lines;
and there my soul keeps sacred tryst
with him whose love upon me shines.
  In gracious words and deeds I view
  his ancient beauty, ever new.

2 I see his glory in the Cross,
displayed in perfect sacrifice:
where love, in life's divinest loss,
has paid its full and costly price.
  Where shame, transformed, with beauty glows;
  and death to life immortal grows.

3 I see his glory in the life
of saint, apostle, martyr, child.
The hero spirit's holy strife;
the tender grace of mercy mild.
  Each life, a mirror of the Lord,
  reflects his lineaments adored.

4 O glory passing human praise;
in book, in Cross, in life revealed;
upon his loveliness I gaze,
and find my soul's diseases healed.
  Till, by his Spirit's grace restored,
  I bear the image of my Lord.

November 1949

Tunes CAREY'S WELLS

A HYMN OF PEACE

What holy strain is swelling
  down growing generations?
its theme of peace,
love, hope, release,
a gracious message telling
to earth's discordant nations.

2 This music God created.
The morning stars, rejoicing,
  together sang
  till heaven rang
in chorus unabated,
their perfect concord voicing.

3 Then why, with harsh intrusion
of hatred, strife and madness,
  should we destroy
  God's peace and joy,
put order in confusion,
and cast o'er life death's sadness?

4 O sin! God's work undoing,
to mar his love's creation;
  his trust betray,
  his image slay;
in blood our hands imbruing.
Deserve we not damnation?

5 But God's love is unbounded,
   for over hate victorious,
     the crucified,
     forgiving, died,
   and on that mercy founded
   is peaceful kingdom glorious.

6 Then lift up hearts and voices,
   with heaven's music blending.
     let love increase,
     forgiveness, peace;
   till all mankind rejoices
   in concord never ending.

May 1950

Tune   BURNLEY WOOD (*W.B. Wordsworth*)

CHRISTMAS HYMN

O day of joy, with holy peace surrounded,
   in quiet beauty dawning on the earth;
bringing glad news of heavenly love unbounded,
   God's blessed tidings of a Saviour's birth.

2 O happy dawn on night of glory breaking,
     when angel music gladdened shepherd ears;
   Israel's hopes to high fulfilment waking;
     ending the evil reign of sin and tears.

3 Down the long ages rings the song of gladness;
     Round all the world the joyful news is borne.
   Peoples that walked in death's dark night of sadness
     hail with rejoicing Jesus' advent morn.

4 Lord, where the smoke of furnaces ascending
     hides earthly sunlight from the worker's eyes;
   let your light shine, the gloomy shadows rending;
     come in your glory, on man's darkness rise.

5 When sin man's soul in blacker night is veiling
     where fear and hate his peace and life destroy;
   send out your light, that over sin prevailing,
     dawned with the angels' advent song of joy.

6 Come! let us join the heav'nly choirs rejoicing:
     draw near to kneel with shepherds and adore.
   'Glory to God' our songs of worship voicing,
     'Peace on the earth' to men for evermore.

August 1950

Tune   ST OSYTH

Spirit, whose first creative word
banished the gloom of ancient night,
still in this book thy voice is heard,
bidding man's darkness turn to light.

2 Thine is the living word that springs
keen as a sword from sacred page;
piercing the inmost soul, it brings
judgment on sin to every age.

3 Thine is the truth that lights the mind
groping amid life's mystery.
Here in thy holy book we find
lamp for the path that leads to Thee.

4 Thine is the saving word that gives
peace to the sinner's troubled heart.
Tidings are here that Jesus lives,
hope to awake and grace impart.

5 Thine is the great world-shaking voice
kingdoms shall hear and cease to be.
Yet in thy promise we rejoice,
ever abiding safe in thee.

July 1951

Tune ANGEL'S SONG

*Written for the occasion of the publication of the
Revised Standard Version of the Bible*

MANSFIELD CHAPEL   JUNE 1951

Within these quiet sanctuary walls
    we seek, O Lord, thy face;
where, like the sunlight's benediction, falls
    the blessing of thy grace.
Each soaring column bids our souls aspire
    to meet thee and adore.
Grant us, O God, the joy our hearts desire
    thy presence evermore.

2 Here sacred memories upon us throng;
    O blessed company.
Here saintly souls inspire us to be strong
    in faith and charity:
and as with loved companions we unite
    in converse, praise and prayer;
the fellowship of saints who dwell in light
    grant, Lord, we ever share.

3 Here beauty glorifies in carven stone
    her maker and her Lord:
while music joins her voice, the name to own
    above all names adored.
Then let us lift up heart and mind and voice
    a living offering;
and with thy church in earth and heav'n rejoice
    our worship, Lord, to bring.

July 1951

Thy Word unchanging speaks to every age;
    all else may change, the kingdoms wax and wane:
still firm endures, above the nations' rage,
that word which never goeth forth in vain:

2 Kindling the prophet's tongue with heav'nly fire;
filling the poet's lips with sacred song;
source of the stern lawgiver's holy ire,
burning against men's deed of cruel wrong.

3 Thy perfect Word was spoken in thy Son,
whereof the Gospels tell the truth and grace:
whose Cross of shame mankind's salvation won;
tidings of joy for all our sinning race.

4 Still thou art speaking in this living hour;
one voice in Scripture's thousand tongues is heard.
Grant us thy Spirit's wisdom, light and power
that we may ever hear and keep thy word.

August 1951

Tune FARLEY CASTLE

*Written for the occasion of the publication of the
Revised Standard Version of the Bible*

Eternal God, thine ancient Word
from chaos first created light:
and still thy voice of power is heard,
triumphant over evil's night.
    Thy living Word from sacred page
    abides our hope and heritage.

2 Thy Word awoke the prophet's ire,
to smite injustice, falsehood, greed.
Forever burns its holy fire,
unsparing foe of wrongful deed.
    Thy living Word from sacred page
    abides our judge from age to age.

3 Thy Word incarnate in thy Son
was full of glory, truth and grace:
and in the living Christ has won
love's homage from a ransomed race.
    Thy sacred Word from Gospel page
    brings Christ anew to every age.

4 Thy Holy Spirit's breath of flame
filled praying hearts with faith and power:
and we who bear our Saviour's name
still know thy Spirit's kindling dower.
    Thy quick'ning Word from sacred page
    revives thy people's heritage.

5 Then speak thy Word, O living Lord,
above our cries of hate and pain:
for comest thou with peace or sword,
thy Word goes never forth in vain.
    Bring, Lord, thy Kingdom's glorious age
    to crown the hope of sacred page.

January 1952

*Written for the occasion of the publication of the
Revised Standard Version of the Bible*

O God, who at creation's birth
dispelled the darkness from the deep,
whose Spirit bade the new formed earth
    awaken from her primal sleep:
        we thank thee for thy growing light
        to guide thy people's steps aright.

2   O Truth, whose flame the prophets led;
        whose splendour shames our base desires;
    thy holiest ray, in Jesus shed,
        our souls to worthier quest inspires.
            Then grant us growing light, that we
            more perfectly thy glory see.

3   From thee, O light of life and love,
        all beauty and all virtue shine;
    illuminate us from above,
        until our spirit mirrors thine:
            and while we strive thy will to know,
            let faith increase and vision grow.

4   Not for ourselves alone we pray
        thy growing light, thy Spirit's fire;
    but for all pilgrims on life's way
        who seek thy truth with strong desire:
            that they, with us, may see thy face,
            and know the fulness of thy grace.

5   Then shall this world, so marred by wrong,
        each blackened city, crowded street,
    all peoples who for freedom long,
        thy Kingdom's dawn arise to greet:
            and in thy light, renewed mankind
            thy liberty and peace shall find.

September 1954

Written for the Church of the Growing Light,
Junction Road Congregational Church, Upper Holloway, London

Thine is the Kingdom, the power and the glory;
　　Kingdom of continent, ocean and sky:
power ever pulsing in atom and heart-beat;
　　glory of great constellations on high.

2　Thine is the Kingdom, the power and the glory;
　　　Kingdom of righteousness, beauty and thought:
　　power of the turbine, of aircraft and radar;
　　　glory designer and craftsman have wrought.

3　Thine is the Kingdom of love's strength unconquered;
　　　thine is the power of a crucified life:
　　thine is the glory of Christ enthroned, victor,
　　　risen triumphant from earth's mortal strife.

4　Come in thy glory, O Christ, with thy Kingdom;
　　　visit this world of our sinning and shame.
　　Claim thy dominion in workshop and city;
　　　rule all our life by the might of thy name.

October 1954

*Written in response to an invitation by the Revd H.D. Oliver,
minister of the Church of the Growing Light, Junction Road
Congregational Church, Upper Holloway, London, to submit
hymns with modern metaphors*

Thy first great gift was light,
　　when chaos fled.
By that same light, O God,
　　we still are led.

2　The light that science seeks
　　　springs from thy mind.
　　In thee our groping thoughts
　　　clear vision find.

3　Astronomer and poet
　　　see by thy flame;
　　and spell, in star or song,
　　　thy shining name.

4　Those broadcast waves that bring,
　　　with tireless speed,
　　a vision or a voice,
　　　were first thy deed.

5 In thee is fire of love
    and sacrifice;
  a lamp lit on the Cross
    at costliest price.

6 Yet hatred, fear and greed
    still cloud thy world.
  Must night descend on earth
    in ruin hurled?

7 Our proud machines but haste
    that blackest night;
  except thou guide our steps
    by wisdom's light.

8 Give us thy lamp of truth,
    thy Spirit's fire,
  with courage, wisdom, faith,
    our lives inspire.

9 Then, in thy growing light,
    we shall arise
  to shape the vision seen
    by open eyes.

October 1954

Tune GROWING LIGHT (*Reginald Thompson*)

*Written for the Church of the Growing Light,
Junction Road Congregational Church,
Upper Holloway, London*

In Bethlehem beneath a starry sky,
when shepherds to a stable cave drew nigh,
a babe in manger laid they found,
and bowed their faces to the ground
    in humble adoration:
before the infant Lord they bowed
    in praise and adoration.

2 To Bethlehem came, guided by a star,
three Magi bearing gifts from lands afar:
  with myrrh and frankincense and gold
  their joyful heart's devotion told,
    with humble adoration.
  With joy they offered treasures rare,
    in praise and adoration.

3 Then unto Bethlehem we too will fare,
   to worship at the Saviour's cradle there.
      Our offering of love we bring
      and thankfully rejoicing sing
         in humble adoration:
      with joyful hearts uplift our song
         in praise and adoration.

1954

L iving God, whose love has gathered
  one great people for thy praise;
in the name of Christ united,
   songs of thankfulness we raise:

2 For thy Son, the world's Redeemer,
      bringing freedom, life and light;
   for the gift by Christ imparted,
      all thy Holy Spirit's might:

3 For apostles, saints and martyrs,
      faithful hearts in every age;
   for the brave, who smiting evil,
      warfare of the Spirit wage.

4 Thanks we offer, Lord, for vision
      ever growing year by year:
   knowledge, charity and freedom,
      faith triumphant over fear.

5 Father, lead thy people onward,
      perfect us in unity;
   till thy Church attains her fulness,
      one in Jesus Christ with thee.

September 1955

Tune MARCHING

*Written for the Triple Jubilee of the Lancashire
Congregational Union*

From Cæsar Augustus went forth a decree;
  O the pride and the power of a throne;
that numbered and taxed all his people must be;
  O the pride and the power of a throne.
Then Joseph and Mary from Nazareth came,
in David's own city to set down their name.
  O the pride and the power of a throne.
  O the pride and the power of a throne.

2 Sweet Mary must travel though bearing her child;
     for how cold is the heart of the world:
   and face on her journey the elements wild;
     for how cold is the heart of the world.
   In Bethlehem's inn was no room left to spare,
   but lodged with the cattle was Mary so fair;
     for how cold is the heart of the world.
     for how cold is the heart of the world.

3 And there in a manger her first-born was laid:
     come, behold him, so humble and small.
   For like to the poorest this infant was made:
     come, behold him, so humble and small.
   But one of Rome's millions, the weakest and least,
   his dwelling a stable, with peasant and beast.
     Come, behold him, so humble and small.
     Come, behold him, so humble and small.

4 Yet here lies the Saviour and King of the earth:
     O with reverence, kneel and adore.
   The Son of the Highest, of heavenly birth:
     O with reverence, kneel and adore.
   God's Word comes incarnate to dwell with mankind;
   our Father is seeking his children to find;
     O with reverence, kneel and adore.
     O with reverence, kneel and adore.

5 Then come, all ye people who sorrow and sin;
     for we bring you glad tidings of joy.
   Draw nigh to the stable and enter within;
     for we bring you glad tidings of joy.
   Your Saviour has brought you God's mercy and peace,
   his comfort for sorrow, from sin your release;
     for we bring you glad tidings of joy.
     for we bring you glad tidings of joy.

1955

Tune THEN COME ALL YE PEOPLE (*W.S. Lloyd Webber*)

L ocked in the atom God has stored a secret might,
energy unmeasured hidden deep from human sight;
gift of God for blessing, made by man the tool of fear;
    shall it evermore be so?

2 Cradled with cattle lay an infant weak and small,
    born of humble peasant, with no dwelling but a stall,
    yet that heart was pulsing with the Love that made the stars:
        is it Love with Power too?

3 God, who in lowliness dost manifest thy power,
    shewing forth thy majesty in atom, star and flower;
    glory to thy greatness! we have seen thy love and might,
        perfected in Bethlehem's child.

October 1955

Written for a Carol Competition by the Cambell Youth Centre,
Langley Crescent, Dagenham, Essex

'L o, I am with you alway,' Jesus said:
'with you whom now I send forth in my Name.
Go to the world and by my Spirit led
teach all the nations and my Word proclaim.

2 Feed each man's hunger with the living Bread:
    my love shall keep you and my power defend;
    my truth shall light each lonely path you tread.
    Lo, I am with you alway to the end.'

3 Lord, at thy Word, to all the world we go;
    grant us thy gift of apostolic fire.
    Kindle our zeal with thine own Spirit's glow;
    with holy love for men our hearts inspire.

4 Give us the strength of faith to meet the foe,
    while on thy promise ever we depend,
    for thine unfailing faithfulness we know,
    'Lo, I am with you alway to the end.'

5 'Unto the end'; when comes that glorious day,
    all power in heaven and earth shall be thine own.
    Death shall be conquered, evil pass away,
    thou in thy majesty shalt reign alone.

6   All life shall dwell in peace beneath thy sway,
    in that blest realm to which our hearts ascend;
    with steadfast faith and eager hope our stay,
    for thou art with us alway to the end.

July 1958, revised November 1963

Tune   FFIGYSBREN

*Suggested, in its original form, by an address by Dr John Marsh
at a Communion Service at Mansfield College, Oxford. Revised
at the suggestion of the Revd John Ticehurst.*

For thee, O Lord, our fathers bore
the Cross, condemned to lonely ways.
Thy Word of truth they cherished more
than earthly comfort, wealth and praise.

2   The freedom Christ bestowed they held
    a sacred trust to be maintained;
    and, by thy Spirit's might impelled,
    thy liberty for us they gained.

3   With thankfulness our debt we own
    to hearts courageous under wrong:
    and praise thee, Lord, whose power alone
    in times of trial made them strong.

4   Now this new age thy challenge brings
    to stand with Christ for freedom still:
    that freedom of the soul which springs
    from service only to thy will.

5   Make us thy freemen, then shall we
    be slaves to no self-seeking aim;
    and fear of evil's power will flee
    before the Saviour's mighty Name.

May 1960

Tune   FINNART

Written for the tercentenary of the 1662 Book of Common Prayer

THE CHRISTMAS COMPANY

We sing the Christmas company;
　　the little, lowly company
　　　　when Christ was born.
In Bethlehem a stable-cave
was all the resting-place men gave
to Mary, Joseph and the Boy,
whose coming angels sang with joy
　　　　that holy morn.
　　O blessed company.

2　We sing the Christmas company;
　　an eager, growing company
　　　　whom Christ made one.
　　The shepherds hasted first to see
　　the Child, and worshipped on their knee.
　　Then Magi, led from distant land
　　by star-light, each with gift in hand
　　　　beheld God's Son.
　　　O happy company.

3　We sing the Christmas company;
　　the great and faithful company
　　　　whose hearts God fired
　　in every age to preach his Word,
　　till all the scattered peoples heard:
　　and men rejoiced throughout the earth
　　to sing of Christ the Saviour's birth.
　　　　God's love inspired
　　　that faithful company.

4　We sing the Christmas company;
　　the universal company
　　　　of every race,
　　who celebrate the sacred day
　　when Christ, God's Word eternal, lay
　　an infant, come to save mankind,
　　that we his peace and joy may find,
　　　　and know God's grace,
　　　with all his company.

September 1960

AN ANTHEM OF THANKSGIVING AND DEDICATION
For the 350th Anniversary of the Authorized Version of the Bible

Now all our hearts in thankfulness unite,
for in our tongue God's holy Word is spoken;
upon our eyes has shone the world's true Light,
and for our souls the Bread of Life is broken.
  Blest are our eyes to see,
  blest are our ears to hear
 what kings and prophets long desired,
  and did in Christ appear.

2 So let us keep a festival of praise,
with joyous anthems of commemoration,
for servants of God's Word in former days
who gave his holy book to bless our nation.
  Blest was the scholar's task,
  the hearts God's Spirit stirred,
 from ancient tongues to English speech
  to bring the living Word.

3 Then with thanksgiving we will bring our vow
God's precious Word within our hearts to cherish,
and seek his grace our spirits to endow
that knowledge of his Word may never perish
  from our beloved land,
  but lighten every shore,
 till all men in God's glory live,
  rejoicing evermore.

November 1960

CHRISTMAS THOUGHTS

One star-lit eastern night
    angelic heralds sang;
on trembling shepherds shone a light,
    while heaven with music rang.
        That holy night
    men knew that God was near.

2   But in the roar and glare
    of our world's crowded life;
its tumult, strain and anxious care,
    its fear and cruel strife;
        how hard it is
    to know that God is near.

3   Yet when the Son of God
    lay in a manger bare,
a heedless crowd around him trod
    and saw no glory there.
        They knew it not,
    but God was very near.

4   Then grant us Lord the sight
    thy glory now to trace,
still shining in the holy light
    of Christ our Saviour's face:
        in him to find
    thy presence always here.

March 1961

*The Choir at Crookham Parish Church, near Aldershot,
sang this hymn as an anthem, to a tune composed by the
Church organist, B.A. Macilroy, on the occasion of the
baptism of Albert's great nephew.*

Praise and thanksgiving
Father, we offer,
for all things living
  you have made good.
    Harvest of sown fields,
    fruits of the orchard,
    hay from the mown fields,
    blossom and wood.

2 Lord, bless the labour
We bring to serve you,
that with our neighbour
  we may be fed.
    Sowing or tilling,
    we would work with you;
    harvesting, milling,
    for daily bread.

3 Father, providing
food for your children,
your wisdom guiding
  teaches us share
    one with another,
    So that rejoicing
    sister and brother
    may know your care.

4 Then will your blessing
reach every people;
each one confessing
  your gracious hand.
    When you are reigning
    no-one will hunger,
    your love sustaining;
    fruitful the land.

June 1961

Tune BUNESSAN

For life and love, for joy and health,
and all the soul's immortal wealth,
our thanks and gifts, O Lord, we bring
to pledge our heart's true offering.

2 Our strength of limb or skill of hand,
our mind thy truth to understand,
thou gavest, Father, to fulfil
the service of thy loving will.

3 In all our toil the vision give
of that high end for which we live,
to praise thee, as by love we show
the grace that, Lord, to thee we owe.

April 1958 (verse 1), October 1961 (verses 2 and 3)

Tunes FESTUS WAREHAM WINCHESTER NEW

Verse 1 was written as an Offering Dedication verse.
The other verses were added for the Eccleston, St Helens,
Congregational Church Christmas Fair

L ord, whose love in humble service
bore the weight of human need,
who didst on the Cross, forsaken,
  work thy mercy's perfect deed:
we, thy servants, bring the worship
  not of voice alone, but heart;
consecrating to thy purpose
  every gift thou dost impart.

2 Still thy children wander homeless;
    still the hungry cry for bread;
  still the captives long for freedom;
    still in grief men mourn their dead.
  As, O Lord, thy deep compassion
    healed the sick and freed the soul,
  use the love thy Spirit kindles
    still to save and make men whole.

3 As we worship, grant us vision,
    till thy love's revealing light,
  in its height and depth and greatness
    dawns upon our quickened sight;
  making known the needs and burdens
    thy compassion bids us bear,
  stirring us to tireless striving
    thine abundant life to share.

4 Called from worship unto service
    forth in thy dear Name we go,
  to the child, the youth, the aged,
    love in living deeds to show.
  Hope and health, goodwill and comfort,
    counsel, aid and peace we give,
  that thy children, Lord, in freedom
    may thy mercy know, and live.

June 1961

*This hymn, revised as above by the Hymn Society of America,
was chosen by the Society as Conference Hymn for the second
National Conference on the Churches and Social Welfare,
October 1961*

L ord of all good, our gifts we bring to thee,
use them thy holy purpose to fulfil;
token of love and pledges they shall be
that our whole life is offered to thy will.

2 We give our mind to understand thy ways,
hands, eyes and voice to serve thy great design;
heart with the flame of thine own love ablaze,
till for thy glory all our powers combine.

3 Father, whose bounty all creation shows,
Christ by whose willing sacrifice we live,
Spirit, from whom all life in fulness flows,
to thee with grateful hearts ourselves we give.

September 1962

Tune CHILTON FOLIAT

Written for Eccleston Congregational Church, St Helens, Christmas Fair

BAPTISMAL HYMN

F ather, thy life-creating love
this sacred trust to parents gave.
in Christ, thou camest from above
thy children's souls to claim and save.

2 Grant, Lord, as strength and wisdom grow,
that every child thy truth may learn.
impart thy light, that each may know
thy will, and life's true way discern.

3 Help us who now our pledges give
the young to train and guard and guide,
to learn of Christ, and so to live
that they may in thy love abide.

4 Then child and home, kept in thy peace,
and guarded, Father, by thy care,
will in the grace of Christ increase,
and all thy Kingdom's blessings share.

November 1963

Tune MELCOMBE

A HYMN FOR THAXTED

Lord, from whom beauty, truth and goodness spring,
world beyond shining world proclaims thee King;
earth in her life and loveliness displays
thy Spirit's presence and declares thy ways.
With all creation we our worship bring.

2 For all the splendour changing seasons hold,
snowfields of winter, autumn's harvest gold,
spring's life resurgent, summer's feast of flowers,
morn's waking glory, calm of evening hours,
our thanks, O Father, ever must be told.

3 Dwelling in this fair town upon a hill,
spire soaring high beside an ageing mill,
homes bowed with years along a curving street,
down to the Guildhall where old highways meet;
where faithful hearts adored, we worship still.

4 Thine are the riches of our heritage,
music and dance, carved stone and author's page.
Thine too the gifts of home and faithful friends,
joys of true comradeship thy goodness sends,
while in thy service, Father, we engage.

5 Chiefly we praise thee for immortal joy
Christ gives and nevermore can death destroy:
joy of eternal fellowship with thee,
this life's sweet foretaste of the life to be,
when praise will ever all our powers employ.

February 1963

Tune BROOMFIELD (*Ruth Bennett and Joy Ashford*)

HARVEST ANTHEM

Let us sing the joy of harvest;
harvest of the earth:
day fulfilling human toil,
sowing, tilling of the soil;
day of promise in the seed,
God will meet his children's need.
Now he makes, by rain and sun,
promise and fulfilment one.

2 Let us sing the joy of harvest;
harvests of the soul:
fruits the Holy Spirit bears
when his grace our heart prepares,
fruits of faith and love and peace,
joys that deepen and increase;
God brings forth, through toil and tears,
harvests for eternal years.

3 Let us sing the joy of harvest;
    harvest at time's end.
God's creative work is done,
crowned with victory his Son.
Gathered by redeeming love,
all his own rejoice above.
Evil's tares his power destroys;
sing then heaven's harvest joys.

March 1964

Thy greatness is like mountains, Lord;
    high as the peaks above:
and like the waters deep and broad,
    the ocean of thy love.
As isles encompassed by the sea
enjoy a blest tranquillity,
    so, girded by thine arm,
    we dwell secure from harm.

2 As sunlight on the lofty hills,
    or star-lit sky at night;
the glory of thy presence fills
    our souls with gracious light.
As river flowing swift and wide,
by torrents from the hills supplied;
    thy Spirit's coming brings
    life from unfailing springs.

3 Fairer than heather on the moor,
    we see in Christ thy face.
As harvest bounty to the poor,
    thy wealth of saving grace.
As soaring eagle upward flies,
our souls on wings of faith arise,
    thy mercy to adore
    in worship evermore.

August 1964

Tune INVERESK

This hymn was first sung publicly by the Linn Choir (Glasgow) at Stirling Festival Concert, 17 May 1965

GETHSEMANE

There is a garden whither Jesus came,
Gethsemane, where olives grow, by name;
the place of testing, where the Holy One
prayed, 'Father, not my will, but thine be done.'

2 This was the place of truth, for grimly clear,
love saw the day of sacrifice draw near;
obedience pointed sternly to the Cross,
where life for all must spring from one life's loss.

3 The place of testing for his men was there,
the truth of all their weakness they must bear;
for they had disobeyed their Master's call
to bear their cross when he for them bore all.

4 Our testing place is here, when truth makes plain
that we have shunned our cross with all its pain,
forsaken Christ, and wholly failed to pay
the price of full obedience in his way.

5 We too deny him, and leave unfulfilled
the costly tasks and mission he has willed.
Forgive us, Lord, and make thy Church the place
where we may find the healing of thy grace.

May 1965

*Suggested by the London Missionary Society sermon preached by the
Revd R. W. Hugh Jones at the Congregational Union Assembly in
Westminster Chapel in May 1965*

'Go into all the world':
clear was the Master's call;
sending his men to give
good news of God to all.
Then forth they went to preach his Word;
land after land their tidings heard.

2 Age after age the Lord
summoned his Church anew;
age after age his realm
greater and wider grew:
till now a myriad tongues confess
his glory, and his Kingdom bless.

3 Rings out his call today,
rousing his Church again;
sends her to tell the world
he comes to save and reign:
man's crowded life he shall control,
and with his Spirit fill the whole.

4 Christ shall mankind unite,
love his design fulfil,
science his truth declare,
power shall obey his will.
his might to save, his right to claim
this great world's life we now proclaim.

February 1966

Tune LITTLE CORNARD

Eternal God, in every place
we find thee where thy people go;
for Christ is there, and in his face
thy glorious light and love we know.

2 As we have seen that glory shine
in hallowed walls, where faithful hearts
long worshipped in a well-loved shrine,
and found the grace thy love imparts:

3 So now we pray that these new walls
may know thy presence, and that here
the light that guides, the voice that calls,
may show thy people thou art near.

4 Here may the past its treasures give
to bless and serve the present age;
and we, entrusted with them, live
to build the future's heritage.

5 As human gifts and skill and love
raise here a house that firmly stands,
so may thy Spirit from above
create a house not made with hands.

March 1966

Tune CHURCH TRIUMPHANT

*Written for the new Baptist Church at Waterlooville,
Hampshire, at the request of the author's sister, and sung
at the stone-laying ceremony on 30 April 1966*

When the morning stars together
their creator's glory sang;
and thy sons, O God, all shouted,
till with joy the heavens rang;
then thy wisdom and thy greatness
their exultant music told,
all the beauty and the splendour
which thy mighty works unfold.

2 When, in synagogue or temple,
voices raised the Psalmists' songs,
offering the adoration
which to thee alone belongs:
when the singers and the cymbals
with the trumpets praised thy care,
all the people saw thy glory
fill the sacred house of prayer.

3 Voice and instrument in union
    through the ages spoke thy praise;
plainsong, tuneful hymn or anthem
    told thy faithful, gracious ways.
Choir and orchestra and organ
    each a sacred offering brought;
while, inspired by thine own Spirit,
    poet and composer wrought.

4 Lord, we bring our gift of music;
    touch our lips and fire our heart;
teach our mind and train our senses;
    fit us for this sacred art.
Then, with skill and consecration,
    we would serve thee, Lord, and give
all our powers to glorify thee,
    and, in serving, fully live.

March 1966

Tune   PICKERING   (*L.H. Bristol Jr.*)

*Written at the invitation of the President and senior class
of Westminster Choir College, Princeton, USA*

Tell me the mysteries you see,
    searching the star-sown night:
probing the sky's immensity,
    out to the bounds of sight.
        Greater the marvel I can show;
            he by whom worlds were made,
        rests in a manger cradle low,
            humbly with cattle laid.

2 Tell me the thoughts that fill your mind,
    learned philosopher:
seeking the pearl of truth to find,
    wisdom which cannot err.
        Come, follow me to Bethlehem;
            kneel with the Magi three;
        worship the Child, and see with them
            wisdom in Deity.

3 Show me the beauty men have wrought,
    stirred by the Spirit's fire:
clothing in sound and colour, thought;
    shaping the soul's desire.
        See God's eternal beauty shine!
            Splendour in flesh arrayed;
        light of incarnate Love divine,
            Godhead in man displayed!

4 Tell me, O men, your cares and toil,
    workers at lathe and loom:
wresting your food from sea or soil,
    risking the miner's tomb.
        Here in a worker's home is One
           destined your road to tread:
        God in a village craftsman's son
           toiling for daily bread.

5 Brother or comrade, husband, friend,
    tell me the love you bear:
reckon the cost of martyr's end,
    measure a mother's care.
        Costlier love you here shall find;
           God's own beloved Son;
        born that the souls of all mankind
           may by his grace be won.

November 1952

Written for a competition for a modern carol in the
SCM for Schools Broadsheet. Awarded the prize
and published in the December 1952 issue

God of the star-fields,
  sown with light's splendour;
thy Word afar wields
  infinite sway.
    Yet in a stable,
    born of a virgin,
    infant in manger,
      thy greatness lay.

2 Seraphs before him
  cried 'Holy, holy';
swift to adore him,
  serving his will,
    now in a manger,
    cradled with cattle,
    only poor shepherds
      worship him still.

3 But now, behold them!
  Magi come riding,
wisdom has told them
  here they will find
    King of the nations,
    Lord of all creatures,
    ruler and Saviour,
      hope of mankind.

4 Hell's might defying,
  see him go fearless
to his cross, dying,
  love's sacrifice.
    Then to his rising,
    sin and death conquered,
    for our redemption
      costliest price.

5 Praise and devotion
  bring him, O peoples!
Sky, earth and ocean
  hail him as Lord.
    For, above all names,
    his, the most worthy,
    by all creation
      shall be adored.

September 1957

Tune BUNESSAN

A 20TH CENTURY CAROL
CHRIST IN A DISPLACED PERSONS' CAMP

Crowded was the camp and cheerless,
where the mourning exiles waited
through the frozen winter night.
One star only, shining peerless,
pierced the gloom with gracious light.

Homeless hearts, I bring good tidings,
God has visited your exile,
comes to dwell with you this morn,
in your midst a Child is born.

2 In the darkness came a maiden
with her spouse, footsore and weary,
homeless by man's harsh decree.
Fair the maid with God's gift laden,
Saviour Child to set men free.

Homeless hearts ...

3 Room and rest the exiles found them,
took the strangers in and fed them,
knowing not they housed their Lord,
till, with God's love shining round them,
lost in wonder, they adored.

Homeless hearts ...

December 1958

Written for a competition in The Sunday Times

A CAROL FOR THAXTED

Let carols ring down ancient ways;
gloria, sing gloria.
By lamp-lit homes your Noels raise,
unbar the gates and doors with praise;
sing gloria in excelsis.

2 By gabled cottage, frosty lawn,
gloria, sing gloria.
At doors green holly wreaths adorn,
repeat the tidings 'Christ is born',
sing gloria in excelsis.

3 Beside the Guildhall's shining tree
gloria, sing gloria.
And down the hill, where flowing free
the little Chelmer seeks the sea,
sing gloria in excelsis.

4　Beneath the Church's soaring spire
　　　gloria, sing gloria.
　　Your songs ascending even higher,
　　for Christmas joys your hearts inspire,
　　　sing gloria in excelsis.

5　Your songs bring succour to man's need;
　　　gloria, sing gloria.
　　They cheer the sad, the hungry feed,
　　and hearts from earth to heaven lead,
　　　sing gloria in excelsis.

January 1964

*Suggested by evenings with a group carol-singing
at Thaxted in aid of Oxfam*

M ost high and holy Lord,
　by heav'nly choirs adored,
poor is the worship of our heart's devotion.
　　Thy truth must light our mind,
　　else to thy glory blind;
　thy love revive the embers of emotion.

2　　Kindle our tongues with fire,
　　　words of true praise inspire,
　　tune them to heaven's songs of adoration.
　　　Take the musician's art,
　　　grace to his soul impart
　　to move our hearts to willing consecration.

3　　Silence shall praise thee still,
　　　when, musing on thy will,
　　thought fails at mysteries beyond our knowing.
　　　Faith shall our worship be,
　　　offered in truth to thee,
　　by lowly souls in love's obedience growing.

4　　Fulness of perfect praise,
　　　Father, alone we raise
　　when all our powers confess that we adore thee.
　　　Help us that praise to give
　　　as for thy will we live;
　　all life in worship offered up before thee.

February 1965

Tunes　NORTH PETHERTON　DOWN AMPNEY

*This hymn received in 1965 the Free Church Choir Union's
Arthur Berridge award for a hymn on worship*

God, whose majesty outshines
heaven's dome of stellar light,
nature in her vast designs
speaks of thy creative might.
Lord, with reverent awe we bow,
worshipping thy greatness now.

2 Lord of all that lives thou art,
rightful Lord of humankind.
thou dost unto man impart
precious gifts of heart and mind:
best, the power to worship thee,
as thy face in Christ we see.

3 God, whose love incarnate came
in thy Son, mankind to save;
bearing all our sin and shame,
victor at the Cross and grave:
we thy mercy's judgment face,
worshipping thy saving grace.

4 Lord, receive our worship here
when our praise in song we bring:
as our hearts in prayer draw near,
take our silent offering;
with the worship crowning all,
lives obedient to thy call.

February 1965

*Written for the Free Church Choir Union
competition for a hymn on Worship*

FOR YOUNG PARENTS

Our Father, whose creative love
the gift of life bestows,
each child of earthly union born
thy heav'nly likeness shows.

2 Grant those entrusted with the care
of precious life from thee,
thy grace, that worthy of the gift
and faithful they may be.

3 Teach them to meet the growing needs
of infant, child and youth;
to build the body, train the mind
to know and love the truth:

54

4 And, highest task, to feed the soul
   with Christ, the living Bread;
   that each unfolding life may grow
   strong in thy paths to tread.

5 These parents need thy wisdom's light,
   thy love within their heart,
   bless thou their home, and for their task,
   thy Spirit's grace impart.

February 1966

Tunes ABBEY   BRADFIELD   SOUTHWELL

This faith we hold, who bear the Christian name,
that God our Father, who gave life, is love,
and in the Man of Nazareth he came
to draw our wayward hearts to his above.

2 For us he lived and died, and rose again,
   that we might know the Holy Spirit's fire,
   and we believe that he, the Christ, will reign
   until he shall the whole of life inspire.

3 He bids us shape our living to his will,
   to love, forgive, to serve and reconcile,
   in daily tasks his purpose to fulfil,
   and smite all wrongs that God's fair world defile.

4 Beyond our hopes of this world's life redeemed
   the vision of eternal life shines clear,
   and that great day when every eye shall see
   his universal reign of love appear.

February 1967

Tune WOODLANDS

L ord, whose Son arose the Victor,
  bringing life from Cross and grave;
and, as grain through death is fruitful,
    ever lives the world to save;
through the years we trace thy purpose
    perfected by giving all,
life laid down to find fulfilment
    in obedience to thy call.

2 For the faith of our forefathers
    when thy great command they heard
to proclaim the glorious Gospel
    where no voice had preached thy Word;
for their vision and devotion,
    service and pure sacrifice,
thanks we give, and for the harvest
    gathered at this costly price.

3 Now another summons bids us
    offer this dear heritage
for thy grace from it to fashion
    new designs for this new age:
ampler plans to serve thy purpose,
    that thy Church may fully give
all her strength to her whole mission
    and through Christ mankind may live.

4 Grant thy Holy Spirit's wisdom,
    shape our plans to serve thy will;
and, from all laid on thine altar,
    make the Church Christ's Body still:
ready to be spent and broken
    that in all her dying frame
Christ may live, and every people
    find salvation in his Name.

October 1965

Tune AUSTRIA

Written at the suggestion of Mr Austen Spearing,
Financial Secretary of the London Missionary Society,
for the occasion when the Society became part of the
Congregational Council for World Mission, and first sung
at the final meeting of the LMS Board

O Lord of circling planets and all the stars in space,
whose purpose through the ages our reason seeks to trace,
thy greatness awes our spirit, thy faithfulness our heart,
and far beyond conceiving, eternal Love thou art.
No worship can be worthy, no words thy praise complete;
our life's devotion only can be an offering meet.

2 Then teach us in our living thy will to know and do,
and keep us to thy purpose both now and ever true:
by humbleness in service, endurance in our pain,
help us for thee to harvest life's wealth of precious grain.
So fit us by our labours, by suffering and love,
to be thy servants always, here and in heaven above.

3 Before us shines the vision of all creation's goal,
when Christ will fully triumph and rule in love the whole;
when hatred, fear and falsehood and every deed of shame
will yield to his dominion, and all men own his Name,
the Name of him who, dying, endured the Cross and grave
to win us life eternal, and all creation save.

February 1967

Tune THAXTED

This day we keep with thankfulness and joy,
for God has set before his Church an open door,
and we will enter
bearing treasures from the past—
The glorious Gospel of the blessed God,
the heritage of saints, apostles, martyrs
and faithful souls who served in quiet ways—
to be the wealth of future generations,
the glory of the city of our God.

With dedication we will keep this day,
and penitence for sins against God's love.
Forgive us, Father:
fire our hearts with hope and faith;
that, with the promise of our risen Lord
'Lo, I am with you alway', to encourage,
we shall go forth to claim the coming years
for Christ, and all their undiscovered riches
for his eternal realm of love and life.

March 1967

*This anthem was written for the dedication of the new building
of Waterlooville Baptist Church, Hampshire. It was set to music
by Mr William Davies*

A MARRIAGE HYMN

Thy Spirit, Lord, inspires our hearts
to seek through love a fuller life.
Thy wisdom willed the bond that seals
this unity of man and wife.

2 Thy hand has led us to this day;
and now we ask thy guidance still:
may years of ever growing joy
the promise of this hour fulfil.

3 As trust and understanding grow,
with tenderness and mutual care,
may body, mind and heart combine
their treasures in one life to share.

4 Let Christ be Lord of this new home,
to train the child, or cheer the guest;
and make this marriage, by his grace,
a life-long union, truly blest.

February 1968

Tunes FULDA   HERONGATE

A CAROL FOR CHRISTMAS

New life is born
for this new world;
as once in Bethlehem, the House of Bread,
a new born Child was laid in manger-bed,
where shepherds worshipped and the wise were led
to him whose life of love man's hunger fed.
   So in our midst today
   the Christ is born again,
   where humble hearts make room
   he comes anew to reign.

2   New life is born
      for this new world
of roaring city streets and motorways,
where wealth and knowledge fascinate man's gaze,
and quest of power fills his restless days:
where hunger kills and war sets earth ablaze.
   Hope, joy and peace and love
   with Christ anew are born,
   as when of old he came
   on earth's first Christmas morn.

3   New life is born
      for this new world.
Then bring from factory and desk and field
your worship, and your richest tribute yield
to Christ, the Life Divine in flesh revealed,
who comes, the might of God's own love to wield.
    Then science, art and trade,
    man's life in home and state,
    will serve the Christ whose reign
    earth's troubled lands await.

June 1968

A HYMN FOR THE SPACE AGE

Great Lord of this vast universe
of galaxies and space,
our straining vision seeks in vain
    its boundaries to trace.
From earth to moon the space-craft bears
    intrepid men afar,
but still beyond shine distant fires
    from nebula and star.

2 We celebrate the skill that bends
    Earth's forces to man's will;
give us the insight, Lord, to see
    your glory, and be still:
with reverent minds to learn the laws
    that order nature's ways,
and for the purposes they serve
    bring gratitude and praise.

3 Inspire us with the zeal to use
    the knowledge we have won,
that man may gain a fuller life
    and all your will be done.
Then health and freedom, justice, peace,
    will here your rule proclaim,
and man, with all your works, will show
    the glory of your Name.

July 1969

Tune HOLY WELL

Written during the Apollo 11 moon mission

A HYMN FOR SENIOR CITIZENS

We bring you, Lord, the praise that flows
    from years your love has guided;
a thankfulness that ever grows
    for joys you have provided:
for youth with all its zest and mirth,
    its hope and aspiration,
for challenges that tried our worth
    and deeds for emulation.

2 Our praise accept for gift of years
    with brain and body healthy;
for kin and friends whose mem'ry cheers
    the hearts their love made wealthy:
for comradeship in work and play
    and comfort in life's sorrow,
for courage matched to every day
    and hope to face the morrow.

3 We praise you for all present joy,
    for wisdom's store of treasure,
for tasks that fruitfully employ
    our freer hours of leisure:
and most, that all our joy and pain
    have proved your love enfolds us,
and through temptation, toil and strain
    your faithful mercy holds us.

4 So now with faith we wait the hour
    when, life on earth completed,
we cast ourselves upon the power
    that death itself defeated:
the living Christ our hope abides,
    the star that cheered our waking,
now towards another morn he guides
    eternal dawn is breaking.

January 1971

Tune BISHOPGARTH

A JOYOUS FAITH

Joyous is the faith we cherish,
  for our God is Love and Lord;
and in Christ he came to give us
  life with richest treasure stored.

2 Numberless the gifts we owe him,
    full the joys God's goodness sends;
  music, art and nature's glory,
    precious love of kin and friends.

3 All the mysteries that science,
    seeking truth, reveals to man,
  are the signs, in star or atom,
    of the great Creator's plan.

4 Brightest crown of our rejoicing
    is that Christ, who died and lives,
  reigns as victor over evil,
    and his life eternal gives.

5 Though man's selfishness and folly
    seek to stay God's mighty hand;
  Christ in faith and joy sustains us
    and we know his work will stand.

September 1971

A HYMN FOR CONGREGATIONAL-PRESBYTERIAN UNION
IN THE UNITED REFORMED CHURCH

Now let us praise our God,
  who makes his people one.
Sing heartily the deeds
  his gracious hand has done.
Lord of the Church, our joy we tell,
for we in one communion dwell.

2 One heritage we share,
    one Spirit's gift of fire:
  age after age he came
    his people to inspire.
  Come to us now, kindle each heart,
  faith, hope and love, 0 God, impart.

3 Our fathers bore the Cross
    through years of strife and pain;
  they suffered shame and death
    our liberty to gain.
  As they for Christ bore hate and wrong,
  Lord, make our spirit brave and strong.

4 Speak, living voice of God,
    to teach, reform, renew:
  make us a Church, 0 God, .
    ever to Christ more true.
  In him our hearts rejoice to find
  good news of Life for all mankind.

January 1972

Tune   CROFT'S 136TH

SPRINGS OF JOY

Joy wings to God our song,
  for all life holds
    to stir the heart,
    to light the mind
and make the spirit strong.

2 Joy wings our grateful hymn,
    for home and friends
      and all the love
      that fills the cup
  of gladness to the brim.

3 Joy wings to God our praise,
    for wisdom's wealth,
      our heritage
      from every age,
  to guide us in his ways.

4 Joy wings to God our prayer.
    all gifts we need
      of courage, faith,
      forgiveness, peace,
  are offered by his care.

5 Joy wings our heart and voice
    to give ourselves
      to Christ who died
      and, risen, lives
  that we may all rejoice.

July 1972

Tunes   EMLEY MOOR (*Peter Cutts*)
         CAERLAVEROCK (*Caryl Micklem*)

CALL TO MISSION

L ord, we have heard your call,
  as once in Galilee
men heard the Christ and left their boats
  his fishers all to be.
  So, in this troubled world,
  this age of fear and strife,
clear is the summons now to share
  your gift of love and life.

2   Love for all loveless lives
  and hearts in deep despair;
love for the homeless and the wronged
  who need a neighbour's care;
  love for all sinning men,
  whom love alone can free
from evil bonds of self to find
  through Christ true liberty.

3   Life, fullest life, you give
  and bid us make men whole;
healing the sick in flesh and mind,
  awakening man's dead soul.
  Giving the hungry bread,
  the poor a livelihood,
bringing the captive and oppressed
  new hope of life and good.

4   Spirit of living flame,
  who gave apostles power,
kindle your servants to fulfil
  our mission at this hour.
  Teach us to speak for Christ,
  as we your call obey;
fire us to show men by our love,
  the Life, the Truth, the Way.

March 1973 (verse 1 revised 1974)

Tune FROM STRENGTH TO STRENGTH

In the power of God's own Spirit
Jesus entered Galilee;
    with a fire divine aflame,
    unto Nazareth he came;
  bade his people hear the Scripture,
'God's anointing Spirit is on me'.

2   'God has sent me', said the prophet,
    'with good news the poor to cheer,
    news that captives will be free,
    news that eyes now blind will see.
  Health for hearts all bruised and broken;
God's own year of favour now is here'.

3   'True this very day', said Jesus,
    'this the task I must fulfil'.
    Forth he went and through the land
    moved with liberating hand.
  Even though men crucified him,
God's unconquered love shone through him still.

4   Lord, you tell us by your Spirit,
    we all need this news today.
    May our faith and service show
    all the gifts that you bestow—
  joy and health and freedom giving,
Lord, from you, the Life, the Truth, the Way.

June 1975

Tune THE SPAIN (*Cyril Taylor*)

This hymn was first sung at the 1977 Hymn Society Conference
Act of Praise in Salisbury Cathedral

INDUCTION HYMN

Your Spirit, Lord, is calling your people at this hour;
  as you summon us to service, so fill us with your power;
to us, with you here gathered, give steadfastness of soul,
to keep our vows unbroken, our dedication whole;
inspire us with your wisdom, give courage, faith and zeal
to prove by loyal actions our promises are real.

2 We thank you, Lord, for calling your servant to this place;
now grant the inspiration to minister your grace;
a voice to give good tidings; and as, in former days,
the company of Jesus learned here to tell your praise,
so may the preacher's message tell us your truth to share,
and to this generation the glorious gospel bear.

3 We, members of Christ's body, accept his sacred call
    to share with our new pastor in offering to all
    the life that Jesus gives us, a life both full and free,
    delivered by your mercy from sin's captivity,
    to serve by love your Kingdom, to succour human need,
    and with your bread eternal our hungry world to feed.

June 1976 (Revised January 1977)

Tune THAXTED

*Written for the Induction Service of the Revd K.M. Chegwin
at Bury Road United Reformed Church, Gosport*

PARTNERS IN MISSION

Thanks be to God, for Jesus reigns,
    dominion round the world he gains,
where hearts unnumbered own him Lord
and praise supreme to him award.

2 Thanks be to God, his Church has grown
    from seed by faithful workers sown;
    apostles, martyrs, pioneers,
    who toiled and suffered through long years.

3 See now the harvest from their toil,
    good grain has sprung from fertile soil.
    One Church of many tongues and lands
    the sign of Jesus' Kingdom stands.

4 One Body, with one living Head,
    by one eternal Spirit led,
    unites its members to fulfil
    the mission Jesus gives us still.

5 As equal partners in one task,
    prepared to serve as God will ask,
    with joy we answer now his call
    and bring our gifts, our love, our all.

September 1976

Tune GALILEE

*Written for the inauguration of the new constitution of the
Council for World Mission*

HYMN FOR THE RITE OF PENANCE

Your holy love shines on us, Lord,
    and searches us within,
revealing in its piercing rays
    the secret depths of sin.

2 Our pride, untruth and lack of love
     condemn us in your sight;
  with anger, evil thoughts and greed
     exposed in your clear light.

3 But in the heart of Jesus Christ
     we see your mercy glow,
  a love that seeks us through the Cross
     forgiveness to bestow.

4 How shall we render for such love
     a fitting offering?
  A humble and a contrite heart
     is all we have to bring.

5 Accept us, Lord, and we would show
     our penitence is real,
  by deeds that every day we live
     the grace of Christ is real.

October 1976

*Written at the invitation of the Roman Catholic
International Commission on English in the Liturgy,
but not adopted*

GOD'S UNIVERSE

With reverence and wonder we view your work, O God,
  done long ere human footsteps this tiny planet trod;
creating through the ages the galaxies afar,
displaying in their systems the glory of each star,
with rays that span in light-years the distances of space,
and we who read their language, creation's story trace.

2 We look into the atom and find a world within
of energies electric and particles that spin,
with power to build up all things, or destroy the universe;
and ours the choice of bringing a blessing or a curse.
We need, O God, the wisdom to use this power aright,
and make it serve your Kingdom, your realm of love and light.

3 We learn the secret process that brings our life to birth,
with all life holds of knowledge, and all that gives it worth.
We find the hidden forces that work disease or health,
and take earth's buried treasures to multiply our wealth.
But, Lord, we need your mercy, oh, humble now our pride,
and grant your Spirit's teaching, with Jesus Christ to guide.

February 1977

Tune THAXTED

Inspired by Nigel Calder's BBC broadcast and book The Key to the Universe

SACRAMENT OF SERVICE

When Jesus in the upper room
shared broken bread and outpoured wine,
he gave his body and his blood
to make a Covenant divine.
He rose and laid his robe aside
and round his waist a towel tied,
then knelt at each disciple's feet
to wash them, dusty from the street.

2 But Peter in his pride refused
to let his Lord serve as a slave.
Then Jesus taught him to accept
the cleansing that his Master gave;
for only so could Peter be,
said Christ, 'in fellowship with me.'
So, Peter's self-assertion stilled,
he let his Lord do as he willed.

3 'You call me Master and your Lord:
I am', said Jesus, 'as you say,
and I have shown you by this deed
how you must now my will obey.
As I have washed your feet, so do
this service for each other too.
If thus you act, obeying me,
I say, how happy you will be.'

4 Forgive us, Lord, the foolish pride
that shrinks from service such as yours—
the pride that craves for power and fame
and glory that the world assures.
We need your cleansing, Lord, that we
from claims of self may be set free.
As you knelt in your humble deed,
help us to serve each other's need.

August 1977

DOUBLE TRINITY

Teach me, O Father, faith that leaps
to venture boldly at your call;
a faith that firmly stands the shock
when life's disasters fall;
a faith that trusts your love and power
to meet life's challenge every hour.

2 Teach me, O Christ, to look with hope
for all the good you have in store;
the coming of your Kingdom here,
eternal life with you;
a hope that nothing can destroy,
I trust the promise of your joy.

3 Give me, O Lord, your Spirit's fire;
a love that sets my soul ablaze
to tell the greatness of your might
a stricken life to raise;
a love that burns to right all wrong
and makes the weak and broken strong.

August 1977

EASTER CAROL

We sing this day the festival of life:
the Lord is risen!
No more the agony and strife;
from Cross and tomb the Victor brings
his crown, and earth rejoicing sings
her Saviour reigneth:
his life remaineth.

2 We sing the triumph God by love has won:
the Lord is risen!
His deed of sacrifice is done.
The wrath of man has fought in vain
dominion from God's love to gain:
his Kingdom glorious
endures victorious.

3   Then let us keep this time with joyful songs:
             the Lord is risen!
       All praise to Christ the King belongs.
       Now death must yield its power to daunt,
       and sin no more its might may vaunt:
             God's love availeth:
             his life prevaileth.

1977

Tune   EASTER CAROL (*John Wilson*)

The original version (July 1958) gave rise to a setting as an
Easter anthem, 'The Festival of Life' by W.S. Lloyd Webber

ASCENSION HYMN

R ejoice, the Lord of life ascends
   in triumph from earth's battlefield.
His strife with human hatred ends,
as sin and death their conquests yield.
       Alleluia!

2   No more his mortal form we see.
    He reigns invisible but near,
    for in the midst of two or three
    he makes his gracious presence dear.
          Alleluia!

3   He reigns, but with a love that shares
    the troubles of our earthly life.
    He takes upon his heart the cares,
    The pain and shame of human strife.
          Alleluia!

4   He reigns in heaven until the hour
    when he, who once was crucified,
    shall come in all love's glorious power
    to rule the world for which he died.
          Alleluia!

January 1979

THESE WONDERFUL DAYS

We praise you, O God, for these wonderful days,
 with so much to find out and do.
The numberless stars in the night sky amaze—
Does life grow on other worlds too?

2 We wonder how all this creation began,
 and what future centuries hold.
Is all of it part of a marvellous plan?
 What secrets will time yet unfold?

3 The Bible records that your Spirit has made
 this earth and the heavens we see:
and, crowning your work in creation displayed,
 you made us your children to be.

4 Our Father, you give us a mind to explore
 the universe in which we dwell:
with knowledge, Lord, help us to grow more and more
 in wisdom to use your gifts well.

February 1979

Tune CARDIGAN (*Meurig Watts*)

Written for Sing New Songs, *published by the National Christian
Education Council in 1981*

GROWING

Thanks be to God for all that keeps us growing,
 growing in spirit, though the flesh decays:
more truth to fill our treasure-house of knowing,
 visions of glory moving us to praise.

2 Thanks for new friends who bring fresh joy to living,
 thanks for the growing company above;
new tasks demanding ever fuller giving,
 God's never ceasing calls to spend our love.

3 Thanks that we face God's challenge to endurance,
 testing the nerves and fibres of our soul;
thanks for the ever deepening assurance
 God's love will bring us to his destined goal.

4 Thanks be to God, eternal life bestowing,
 building our strength on Christ the living bread,
Christ the true vine, whose life within us flowing,
 quickens the growth of souls whom he has fed.

August 1979

Tunes EASTWOOD STONEGATE HIGHWOOD

RENEWAL

L ord, renew my faith to live
eager to obey your call;
take the best I have to give;
stir my heart to venture all.

2 Teach me for your sake to care
for my fellow-members' needs;
giving neighbours everywhere
timely help in loving deeds.

3 In your mercy I rejoice,
you have given all for me;
I would offer heart and voice
your ambassador to be.

4 Through your church you give me, Lord,
wealth of fellowship and joy:
take my life, in love outpoured,
in your kingdom to employ.

5 Train and use me to proclaim
your deliverance and worth;
till the glory of your name,
Lord and Saviour, fills the earth.

May 1980

Tune HARTS

*Written for the renewal campaign of Christ Church
United Reformed Church, Chelmsford*

THE ROCK AND THE RIVER

'We have made a mistake in calling God the Rock. He is also the River'

We worship God the Rock, unmoved, secure;
like mountains which from ages past endure,
a strong foundation for our faith and life,
our rock of confidence in storm and strife.

2 We worship God the River, flowing fast,
with life-renewing waters sweeping past;
a stream creating good to bless the earth,
and bringing beauty in new forms to birth.

3 We worship God the Rock and River, one;
without the water, life had not begun;
without the rock, the river could not flow;
we find both true, when God we fully know.

June 1980

Tune FARINGDON (*Philip Jones*)

JUSTIFICATION BY FAITH

How glorious is a life set free
to face God's judgment unafraid;
for on the cross of Christ we see
divine forgiving love displayed.

2 In vain we strive this peace to gain,
no life can bear God's holy light,
no effort wipe away the stain
on souls exposed to his pure sight.

3 By faith alone we grasp God's hand
outstretched to draw us to his side;
that by his mercy we may stand
made one with him through Christ who died.

4 Then, God be praised, who freely gives
his people pardon and release;
and happy everyone who lives
to serve this gracious Lord of peace.

March 1981

Creator Spirit, fount of life
and spring of all creative power,
each human art you bring to birth
draws life from you to grow and flower.
Now we this glorious harvest bring,
our worship's grateful offering.

2 We offer music's gift of praise;
its power to move our souls to prayer,
and fire our hearts with faith and love,
your gracious gospel to declare.
We bring the arts of dance and song,
for these to perfect praise belong.

3 This sacred house in which we meet
was by an architect designed
that we might find you present here,
though not by walls to be confined.
We learn within this place of prayer
to recognize you everywhere.

4 The artist, sculptor, carver owe
their gifts to your inspiring grace;
in drama, poetry and prose,
your active Spirit's work we trace.
The Church receives from all the arts
these treasures which your love imparts.

5 Then teach us so to use these gifts
that praise may every power employ,
and all the world be moved to share
the fullness of your people's joy;
for Jesus Christ has come to give
abundant life for all to live.

1981

BRIDGE BUILDING

Lord, who linked your heaven to earth
with a bridge of love divine;
timeless glory, humble birth,
joined in one supreme design;
we would be bridge builders too,
spanning all the world for you.

2 Bridges we would strive to build,
foes transforming into friends,
till this war-torn world is filled
with the peace your Spirit sends;
and, with one united voice,
peoples, freed from fear, rejoice.

3 When, in selfish quest for wealth,
we ignore our neighbour's need;
thoughtlessly enjoying health,
while the helpless vainly plead;
Lord, awaken us to share,
building bridges with our care.

February 1982

Written at the suggestion of the Revd David H. Dale,
minister of Christ Church United Reformed Church, Chelmsford

HERITAGE AND TASK

Father, we have seen your glory
in the light of Jesus' face,
and the sacred gospel story
tells your love for every race.
By your Spirit's inspiration
in your Church from age to age,
we received this heritage.

2 Lord, you give in fullest measure
joys in fellowship to share;
scripture's precious store of treasure,
song and sacrament and prayer;
with the living voice of preacher,
making known your will today,
and your summons to obey.

3 Lord, forgive, we take for granted
these rich gifts that you bestow,
For the church our fathers planted
little thankfulness we show.
We would learn to prize more dearly
our inheritance from you,
and to offer service due.

4 Then, renewed in dedication,
    we shall face the tasks ahead;
till our troubled generation
    to your healing grace is led;
and your liberating Spirit
    brings from hate and fear release,
    with your kingdom's gift of peace.

March 1982

Tune MAYFLOWER (*Caryl Micklem*)

*Written for the United Reformed Church Eastern
Province 'Day Out' at Westcliff, June 1982*

THE FATHER'S GIFTS

*... every perfect gift comes from above, from the Father
of the lights of heaven. With him there is no variation ...*

James 1.17 NEB

We owe you, Father, every gift
    that fills with perfect good our life;
and for this lasting treasure lift
    our song of praise.

2 The shining worlds that light the skies
bear witness to your steadfast mind:
and humbly from our hearts arise
    our songs of praise.

3 For gifts of hearing, sight and brain;
for science, craftsmanship and art,
and skill to heal disease and pain,
    we sing our praise.

4 For Jesus Christ, your Son, our Lord,
your love's most costly gift of all.
and for your Spirit's power outpoured,
    we sing our praise.

5 Great Lord of all the Church on earth,
where pardoned sinners find the wealth
that gives our life eternal worth,
    accept our praise.

6 But not in song alone we bring
our thanks for all your love bestows;
our life must be the offering
    that tells our praise.

April 1982

OUR CHOICE

Spirit of God, your voice
awakens the world today,
facing us with the choice,
which is to be our way?
The road to death through hate and strife,
or love's way through to peace and life?

2 Do we not hear a cry
coming from many lands?
'Why are we doomed to die,
broken by cruel hands ?
While fear creates worse weapons still,
a million human lives to kill.'

3 Church of the Lord, arise!
Heed now the Spirit's call;
answer these hopeless cries—
'God's work shall never fall.
We pledge ourselves to serve him now,
and seek his help to keep our vow.'

4 People of God, unite!
One is the task we share,
strong in the Spirit's might,
love's saving power declare.
Make Christ the whole world's Prince of Peace
and never rest till conflicts cease.

5 Lift up your voice in song;
look for God's promised hour:
Christ will defeat all wrong,
God's kingdom come in power.
Till then, press on, by faith made brave,
our sinning world God wills to save.

September 1982

Tune LITTLE CORNARD

THE RED CROSS

Life-giving Spirit, source of health and joy,
inspiring us to care;
our skill we bring you to employ
and would your service share.
Equip us to respond to human need
with your compassion shining through our deed.

2 Strong was your arm to offer healing aid
through Christ in Galilee:
and on the Cross we see displayed
love free from enmity.
Then fill us with his spirit, that we show
our mercy equally to friend and foe.

3 Bearing his Cross for sign, we hear your call
for love that spares no cost
to succour those who, injured, fall,
the refugee and lost:
to aid the handicapped and old with cheer
and break the bonds of cruelty and fear.

March 1983

Lord Christ, we worship you, the sinner's friend,
baptised with those who heard John's call, 'repent',
companion of the outcast and despised
and crucified with bandits at the end.

2 In humble love you shared our human pain,
our conflicts with temptation, sorrow, hate,
sustained by trust in your own Father's care;
that all of us abundant life should gain.

3 Then, on the Cross, you faced one conflict more,
exceeding all your body's agony,
more cruel than the shame. and mocking cries,
the falsehood and betrayal which you bore.

4 'My God, oh why have you forsaken me ?'
That cry of desolation echoes ours,
when sin hides from our eyes our Father's face,
and we no sign of his compassion see.

5 You sinned not, but our hardest road you trod,
that you might bring us through that agony,
to rise with you, forgiven and restored,
and live in perfect union with our God.

October 1983

We thank you, Lord, for all the gifts
your Spirit on the Church bestows;
the skill to teach, the faith to heal,
each your abounding goodness shows.

2 We thank you that your love inspires
the preacher's word, the pastor's care;
that we may know your saving grace
and all its riches fully share.

3 When we in praise and prayer unite,
your Spirit guides the voice that leads
our hearts to seek and find you near
with bread that all our hunger feeds.

4 The years bring change; our pastor goes
to other tasks; but we retain
a heritage that will not pass,
your Spirit's store of precious grain.

5 When all your people's gifts combine,
the Church becomes a living whole,
with Christ as Head, whose reign of love
is all creation's glorious goal.

February 1984

*This hymn was written for, and sung at, a service of farewell to
David and Betty Dale at Christ Church, Chelmsford, 28 April 1984*

AN EASTER HYMN

L ife is born of death today,
   joy is born of sorrow;
now, where Christ in darkness lay,
   dawns a shining morrow.
      Christ is risen; alleluia!
      Christ is risen from the dead.

2 Love has conquered bitter hate,
    cruelty is forgiven;
sin and death have met their fate,
    from their strongholds driven.
      Christ is risen; alleluia!
      Christ is risen from the dead.

3 Evil deeds would faith destroy,
    still God's love defying;
but within us Easter joy
    glows with flame undying.
      Christ is risen; alleluia!
      Christ is risen from the dead

4 Living Christ, your triumphs bring
    death to wrong and sadness;
we would tell our joy and sing
    our refrain of gladness;
      Christ is risen; alleluia!
      Christ is risen from the dead.

March 1984

Tune MARNHULL (*Michael Dawney*)

*This text, celebrating the conquest over death of life in Christ,
was written shortly before Albert's own death. It was submitted
for an Anglia Television Easter Hymn competition. It was
runner-up and was included in the television broadcast*

The Poems

HOLLINGREAVE

Grey are the houses,
dark are the mills,
tall are the chimneys
by the great hills;
what is the pattern
of life that you weave,
Christ and his people
in your Hollingreave?

Woven of courage,
sacrifice, love,
faith's shining vision
sent from above;
such is the pattern
of life that we weave,
Christ and his servants
in our Hollingreave.

Hearts pure and humble,
hands that are strong,
deeds that are kindly,
laughter and song;
Christ gave the pattern
of life that we weave,
he and his comrades
in our Hollingreave.

Youth that is eager,
age that is wise,
manhood's full vigour,
children's bright eyes;
these make the pattern
of life that we weave,
Christ and his brethren
in our Hollingreave.

Home circles happy,
work done with zest,
play that is healthy,
worship and rest;
fair is the pattern
of life that we weave,
taught by the Master
in our Hollingreave.

Christ the great weaver
stands by his loom,
calls to endeavour
all in the room;
glorious the pattern
of life we shall weave,
Christ and his workers
in his Hollingreave.

1946

*These verses were written as a Christmas greeting
in connection with Hollingreave Congregational Church.
Hollingreave was a cotton-weaving town*

TO ALBERT SCHWEITZER

Schweitzer, thou royal hearted friend of man;
great in the realms of music, healing, thought;
clothing in deeds the wisdom thou hast taught,
shaping thy life to youth's heroic plan;
prophetic soul, whose thinking far outran
the spirit of thine age, and questing, caught
visions of truth humanity has sought
since mind's immortal Odyssey began:

Honour we gladly pay thee; but thy praise
rings strangely in this world of angry strife:
a nobler song of tribute we shall raise
when, from this age with bitter passions rife,
we turn to wiser deeds and kindlier ways,
and keep thy precept, reverence for life.

February, 1948.

This sonnet was inspired by reading Albert Schweitzer,
the man and his mind, *by George Seaver. It was printed in*
The Christian World *on 19 January 1950*

MANSFIELD—TWENTY YEARS ON

Swiftly as racing crews upon the stream,
the craft of memory bear down time's flood:
frail as the magic fabric of a dream,
yet still with power to stir the sleeping blood.
From ageing stones long silent voices call;
remembered faces mingle with the throng;
while faintly on my ears the echoes fall
of earnest discourse and light-hearted song.
Each cadence of the organ's holy strain
is rich with harmonies of other days:
a company far-scattered meets again,
joined with the visible in prayer and praise.
    Lord of the past's immortal heritage,
    let me not mar the future's hidden page.

June 1948

*The Mansfield College Old Men's Meeting inspired these lines,
which appeared in the College Magazine*

IONA

Thou wast the island of Columba's quest;
when, penitent for anger's bloody stain,
he steered his coracle from out the west,
new souls for Christ beyond the sea to gain.
Thou wast the island whence the Light was borne
to Scottish glen and wild Northumbrian moor;
when, in the shining splendour of that morn,
men heard God's joyful tidings for the poor.
Thou art the island where the Word of Life
goes forth again in all its ancient power;
to heal, to build, to fashion peace from strife,
proclaiming Christ and his triumphant hour.
    Iona, thou does bring a prophecy
    of earth, redeemed, made beautiful and free.

July 1948

This sonnet was written as a result of a week with the Iona Community

CHARLES FREER ANDREWS

Christ's faithful apostle

His was the greatness of a humble heart;
the strength of meekness; and the kingly power
resting on service. Wealthy was his dower
of tender lovingkindness: skilled his art
to heal the wounds of hatred, and impart
God's peace to men in their discordant hour.
To all oppressed he was a refuge tower;
feeling of every wrong the bitter smart.

Thus we remember him, and read his fame
inscribed upon the hearts of foes made friends;
the souls of men released from fear and shame:
in lives whose praise the brightest glory lends;
who saw the beauty of his Master's Name
through him, and learned to strive for Christlike ends.

November 1948

*A tablet in memory of C.F.Andrews was unveiled at his birthplace,
14 Brunel Terrace, Newcastle-upon-Tyne, on November 30th, 1948.
These lines were written for the occasion*

THE GREATER GLORY

When in the shining records of the great
I seek the names whose lustre fairest gleams;
I find them not in those whose soaring dreams
exalt them to high office in the state:
nor in the ruthless conquerors who sate
their lust for victory in blood-red streams:
nor men of genius whom history deems
creative architects of human fate.

Far brighter fame illuminates the page
which celebrates the Spirit's pioneers:
who in the strength of God their conflict wage
for love and truth, with blood and bitter tears,
against the Prince of Darkness' evil rage.
Yours is the glory, saints, apostles, seers!

1948

*The above was written for the Celebration 'A Whirlwind for Christ'
which commemorates the great pioneer missionary in Madagascar, William
Kendall Gale. The Celebration was published by the London Missionary
Society*

THE HOLY FAMILY

*Whosoever shall do the will of God,
the same is my brother, and my sister, and my mother*

A carpenter, a mother with her child,
their shelter but the stable of an inn:
an alien world around, unthinking, wild;
so did the holy family begin.
Then led by angel choir and shining star,
shepherds and Magi brought their offering
of praise and gifts from regions near and far,
finding a place within the sacred ring.
The circle widened, heart was linked to heart
from land to land, one holy family,
all brethren of one Lord, no more to part
in all the wideness of eternity.
So you and I may find with Christ a place
within the vast home circle of his grace.

September 1948

A Christmas Sonnet

CHRISTMAS VERSES

*Nothing is so beautiful as a light in a cottage window, except the light of the stars;
and when we feel the beauty of the cottage light, we know that it is of the same nature
as the beauty of the stars—and our desire is to be sure that the stars are the lights of
home with the same spirit of home behind them*

A. Clutton-Brock

A cottage window lit at eventide,
cleaving the dusk with slender shaft of light;
the late returning traveller to guide;
and bearing through the mystery of night
    the spirit of a home.

Uncounted constellations of the sky,
displaying jewelled splendour in the dark;
the blaze of giant nebulae on high
subdued by distance to a single spark.
    Is it the light of home?

A star above a lowly stable door,
where God's own glory shines from infant eyes.
Now are the heavens inscrutable no more:
behold! behind the splendour of the skies
    the spirit of a home.

September 1949

VINCENT DE PAUL

L ove was the fiery torch of Vincent's heart:
love was the incandescence of his eyes:
love was the lamp that made his spirit wise
to see the wounds of men and ease their smart.
Christ gave him mercy's skill, with blessed art
to feed the hungry, still the foundling's cries:
and where the galley-slave, with bitter sighs
toiled at the oar, his arm would strength impart.

O God of love, to whose eternal fire
our human loving owes its humbler flame;
kindle our hearts with Vincent's high desire
to serve the lowliest in Jesus' Name:
nor shall our souls to other place aspire
than where with Christ we share love's cross of shame.

March 1950

The above sonnet was inspired by the film Monsieur Vincent

BETHLEHEM

T here is a quiet town among the hills,
where life's slow pulse marked uneventful years.
The great world heeded not her joys and tears,
nor she the nations' destinies and ills.
But God by lowly means his plan fulfils;
and now from Bethlehem the whole world hears
the bells recall Christ's birth, when shepherd ears
heard news which now all hearts with gladness thrills.

Then humble though thy home, thy life may hold
a blessing for the world of greater worth
than can be priced in perishable gold.
If Christ within thy heart's abode hath birth,
let all thine Advent joy abroad be told,
God's ever new glad tidings to the earth.

A setting of this verse was composed by W. S. Lloyd Webber

EVEREST

Far from the shouting crowd they climbed the height,
by precipice and wind-swept ridge, to scale
the lonely peak, long sought in man's stern fight
o'er elemental forces to prevail.
There on the summit races met, and shared
the glory of heroic enterprise;
and with them triumphed men who long since dared
but failed, who now to victory arise.
Let this be symbol of God's splendid quest,
whereon this Queen and Commonwealth shall gain
the noblest crown, and win their Everest:
that height where equal honour all attain
who humbly serving, Christ's commands fulfil,
and seek, one brotherhood, his perfect will.

June 1953

WINGS

I heard a rush of wings and thought of angels:
looked up, and saw the migrants flying south.
The air vibrated with their beating pinions
pursuing autumn's fast retreating sun.
Around tall trees across the lane's end wheeling,
in crowding rank on rank they dropped to rest:
and every branch was loud with eager music,
shrill with a tumult of ecstatic song.

I heard a rush of wings and thought of angels;
God's choiring heralds of goodwill and peace:
to Bethlehem's astonished shepherds bearing
their joyous tidings of a Saviour's birth.
Then, 0 my soul, mount up on wings of worship;
attune thy voice to heaven's exultant praise;
that earth may hear again the songs of Advent,
those holy strains which first the angels sang.

A setting of this poem was composed by W. S. Lloyd Webber

TO ALBERT SCHWEITZER
For his 80th birthday

Each noble life hath music; lyric song
of piercing beauty, dying soon; or call
to battle, trumpeted in face of wrong;
or solemn notes which from the sufferer fall.
Thy music, Schweitzer, is an ampler strain,
meet for a mighty instrument; thy years
speak, organ-like, a many voiced refrain,
wherein, through change, one glorious theme appears.
Thought, aspiration, action blend their chords
in diapason—reverence for life
the burden of the long years time affords,
all filled with mercy's liberating strife.
    Like Bach, thy soul's immortal music gives
    The harmonies whereby man's spirit lives.

December 1954

SWANLAND

God's house looks forth upon the quiet street,
across the pond where white swans proudly ride,
a well-house, school and village sign, beside
the pool, are clustered where the four roads meet.
Amid such peaceful scenes once moved the feet
of One who, humbly born, was crucified;
but rose that with his own he should abide;
and all the powers of death and sin defeat.

So long ago! So far away! But no;
he walks today unseen our village ways:
and when, at morn or eve, his people go
to break the bread, or offer prayer and praise.
or hear the Christmas tidings told; then, lo!
Their eyes are opened. and upon him gaze.

January 1955

A setting of this poem, entitled He walks unseen, *was composed
by W. S. Lloyd Webber*

Albert Bayly held a pastorate at Swanland, near Hull, from 1950-56

There remaineth therefore a rest to the people of God

From high-arched hilltops warriors saw below
their legionary foemen claim the land.
These rocks, tumultuous with shout and blow,
helped, all in vain, the British tribesmen's stand.
The legions marched away, another hand
ruled hill and valley; yielding power again
to proud invaders from the Norman strand.
Now all is peace: the Gospel's gracious strain
proclaims the King of Love's eternal reign,
while on the hillsides flocks in safety feed.
But strife must still the Christian's lot remain
till love shall over all be Lord indeed.
   Then earth with heaven in one great Sabbath blest
   Shall in the peace of God find perfect rest.

July 1957

Written at The Rest, All Stretton

BEAUTY UNEXPLORED

Three tall spires in the distance,
   set in a valley fair:
often I travel past them,
   never to journey there.
Many a great Cathedral,
   or village House of God
I have seen with treasure of ages stored;
   but summoning clear,
     the call I hear
   of beauty unexplored.

Island hills to the westward,
   under a cloud-flecked sky,
far from the ship's course, rising
   stately, to summits high.
Noble the cliffs and headlands.
   and fair the silver strand
of the isles in memory's precious hoard;
   but urgent and clear.
     the call I hear
   of beauty unexplored.

December 1958

The spires are those of Lichfield Cathedral.
The islands are some of the Western Isles of Scotland

THE HILLS OF ENGLAND

I sing the hills of the South land,
  from Wessex to Weald of Kent:
the springy turf of the downland,
  with bracing, pungent scent.
Thank God for the gift of the chalk land,
  white cliff and gorse and Ring;
for ancient barrow and beacon—
  the hills of the South I sing.

I sing the hills of the North land,
  Northumbria's fortress wall:
the grey, steep crags of the Border,
  and heather's purple pall.
Thank God for the hills of the North land,
  great Cheviot, Simonside;
for wind-swept summit and moorland,
  the Ottercops wild and wide.

I sing the hills of the West land,
  from Malvern to Devon shores:
of Cotswolds fair and the Mendips;
  and Dartmoor's rocky tors.
Then East I will sing of the Clevelands,
  of Yorkshire moors and Wolds;
for all show forth in their beauty
  the treasure our island holds.

Thank God who gave us this England,
  with hills for her crown and pride:
the Pennines, Peak to High Cross Fell,
  with Pendle and Great Whernside:
and, noblest, the summits of Lakeland,
  Helvellyn, Scafell tall—
I lift my eyes to the hilltops
  in praise to the Lord of all.

November 1958, revised 1960 and 1966

GULLS

I have thrilled to the notes of a blackbird's song,
    the moorland curlew's cry,
a lark's long throbbing ecstasy
    flooding the summer sky.
But the call that stirs my heart,
    and sets my eyes alight,
is the wild call, the haunting call,
    of gulls in soaring flight.

For it calls me afar to the towering cliffs,
    and rocks where great seas break;
to islands lost in summer haze,
    ships with a foaming wake:
where the gulls in grey and white,
    upborne on tireless wing,
with a wild cry, a haunting cry,
    in ceaseless circles swing.

December 1958

CHEVIOT LANDSCAPE

Heather's out on the hillside;
    purple cloak cast round
the shoulders broad and arms outflung
    of moors green gowned.
Heather borders the farm-track
    climbing over the ridge
to a lonely house by wind-swept trees,
    and the burn beneath a bridge.

Hives are up on the heather:
    honey calls the bees.
The tall grass sings and bracken bows
    before the breeze.
Fleeting shadows of cloud-ships
    race from valley to hill:
and the winds from God's wide spaces give
    of their life my soul to fill.

September 1960

A setting as a part-song entitled Heather Hills
was composed by W. S. Lloyd Webber

NORTHERN HILLS

Long have I loved these northern hills,
　　stately and fair their form;
sunlit under a summer sky,
　　dark in a winter storm.

Hills of the north, your beauty calls,
stirs in my heart a sleeping fire,
wakens the deep untamed desire
　　to roam your heights again.

Cheviot, Hedgehope, Yeavering Bell,
　　heather and bracken gowned;
Coquet River and College Burn,
　　tumbling with cheerful sound.

Hills of the north ...

Long is the line of Pennine heights,
　　Cross Fell to Kinder Scout;
wild the waters that hurtle down
　　High Force and Caldron Snout.

Hills of the north ...

East to the Moors and Cleveland Hills,
　　south to the Yorkshire Wolds,
west to Pendle and Pen-y-ghent,
　　farmsteads and lonely folds.

Hills of the north ...

Noblest of all, the Lakeland fells
　　rise up in royal pride;
Scafell Pike and Great Gable stand
　　towering side by side.

Hills of the north ...

February 1962

LIVERPOOL CATHEDRAL
April 1961

Still grows the noble fabric: stone on stone
sets forth the beauty of the great design.
Creative thought and manual skill combine
to praise the living Spirit, who alone,
in glory reigning from the triune throne,
endowed the builders with a gift divine,
to raise in majesty and grace a shrine
where God may hold communion with his own.

This great cathedral, now so stately grown
in chancel, tower, nave, shall be a sign
of that eternal city which remains
unchanged by time, where God is fully known;
for in her midst his light doth ever shine
and over her the risen Saviour reigns.

April 1961

Written after the opening of the first bay of the Nave

MANSFIELD COLLEGE OXFORD
Opening of new residences by Her Majesty Queen Elizabeth the Queen Mother
June 25th 1962

Here life is shaped for service by the Word
that first created light, and gave the flame
of truth to prophets of the sacred Name,
who saw God's glory and his judgments heard.
That Holy Spirit who Apostles stirred
the saving might of Jesus to proclaim,
comes here in power, as of old he came,
his servants for their ministry to gird.

These doors now opened by a royal hand
shall be a gateway for the King of Kings;
that young lives, hearing the command he brings,
shall learn to bear his truth from land to land:
till from the good seed of the Gospel springs
a Kingdom's harvest that shall ever stand.

May 1962

Read by the Principal, Dr John Marsh, at the Opening Ceremony

Here is the place where God's hand shapes again
the living clay by cruel diseases spoiled;
and from the midst of injury and pain
brings forth the comeliness that evil foiled.
Here heaven's wisdom uses human skill,
and Christ's compassion moves man's heart to care.
Here surgeon's knife and nurse's hands fulfil
God's plan the wasted tissues to repair.
Here death is challenged by resurgent life,
and love puts all despair and fear to rout:
as, disciplined and girded for their strife,
the conquerors of suffering go out.
   This house of healing is a holy place,
      where dwells the Lord of life in kingly grace.

September 1962

THAXTED

A secret beauty here in Thaxted dwells
that holds my heart in strong devotion bound:
not in the majesty of peaks and fells
   nor in the mystery of ocean found.
But when in spring the fields are green with corn
   my spirit with ascending lark takes wing:
the flame of autumn, evening light and dawn
   on spire and ancient walls their treasures bring:
and, fairer still, the grace of quiet lives
   bright with the beauty of true holiness:
a company made one by love that strives
   to offer Christ, who came this world to bless,
the music of a worship that displays
   all heaven's beauty perfected in praise.

September 1964

PEACE IN THAXTED

Peace, deep peace, the peace of God is here,
  peace of the hills that far as eye can see,
like a still image of the ocean swell,
    rest in their ancient quietness.

Peace, God's peace, when spring awakes to life
crocus and aconite and snowdrop pure,
daphne and daffodil and violet,
    first of earth's beauty blossoming.

Peace, deep peace, the song of moonlit brook,
peace of night's quiet streets and lamplit homes,
under the planets and far galaxies,
    glory of God's own majesty.

Peace, God's peace, where love indwells a home,
making a sanctuary for tired souls:
peace in communion of dear friends who share
    treasures of life in fellowship.

Peace, deep peace, within the House of God,
voices and hearts in unison of praise,
while a skilled touch upon the organ keys
    summons all heaven's harmony.

Peace, deep peace, the peace of God is here.
As I have found this peace, so let me give
peace to all troubled hearts, all strife-torn souls,
    peace that is life's true blessedness.

May 1963

THE STEPS, THAXTED

Here was great music born: these walls have heard
new strains spring living from creative thought.
Here song and symphony took shape, and brought
a strange new beauty to the hearts they stirred.
The music-maker clothed the poet's word
in robes of sound of finest texture wrought;
austerely strong, with mind's rich burden fraught;
a mind no fear of human blame deterred.

Such was the man we honour here: his name
adds glory to this town's rich heritage:
and we, who now in Thaxted's story claim
for Gustav Holst a fair, immortal page,
would learn from him, and all he gave, to aim
with like integrity to serve our age.

July 1963

*Written for the unveiling, on July 5th, 1963, of a plaque on the Manse
(formerly The Steps), Town Street, Thaxted, recording the residence there of
Gustav Holst from 1917-25. The sonnet was read at the ceremony by
Sir Adrian Boult, who unveiled the plaque*

TO A YOUNG BLUE-TIT

A tiny ball of beauty, brown and blue;
soft plumage, quickly beating heart, bright eyes,
and flutt'ring wings that never fully knew
the joy of freedom from the earth to rise.
Your days were few. You came from sheltered nest
to find the world for your frail life too hard:
the care of parents failed. You found no rest
till human hands became your friend and guard:
too late to give a bird's full span of years:
but not in vain did your brief moments speed:
we saw your loveliness. We knew the joy and tears
of caring and compassion for your need.
    You passed, but left us for eternal gain
    your beauty in our hearts to heal our pain.

June 1965

This tit, rescued by Miss Ruth Bennett of Thaxted, died after a few days

Such music have I heard in this fair place,
　such gracious music heard:
a tumult of bird voices greeting dawn,
the throbbing ecstasy of rising lark,
the tiny ringing hammer stroke of tits
and pure, clear notes of robin, dunnock, wren;
song-thrush and blackbird's modulated phrase,
consoling pigeon and shrill piping swift;
one symphony of richly woven sound.
　　Such music have I heard,
　　harmonious music in this place.

Such music have I heard in this fair place,
　　such joyful music heard:
bells pealing to proclaim that Christ is born,
gay carollers around the Guildhall steps,
and in crisp snow, lamp-lit from friendly homes;
in summer, madrigals upon the lawn;
the jingling steps of merry Morris-Men;
and country dancing to gay English airs
or Scotland's 'Ships of Grace' and lively reels.
　　Such music have I heard,
　　heart-cheering music in this place.

Such music have I heard in this fair place,
　　such precious music heard
within the sanctuary when voices blend
in adoration, thankfulness and prayer;
and sensitive to skilled musician's touch
the organ's many voices speak the strains
of Mozart, Elgar, Beethoven and Bach:
or when a choir and orchestra unfold
the themes of Holst and Verdi's Requiem.
　　Such music have I heard,
　　most sacred music in this place.

Such music have I heard in this fair place;
　　the living music heard
of merry laughter from a child at play;
in kindly welcome by a trusted friend;
chords of endurance and deep rooted faith;
the wordless music of a humble life,
wherein the harmonies of truth and love
make one great symphony of perfect praise,
a soul's pure adoration of her Lord.
　　Such music have I heard,
　　life's holiest music in this place.

June 1965

I looked for Christ in Thaxted.
I sought him in the fields at dawn,
   and knew he passed that way;
 for he had multiplied the corn,
and on the seed that dies to live again
the marks of his own sacrifice were plain.

I looked for Christ in Thaxted.
I sought him where men toil and trade
   in factory and shop;
 and he by whom the worlds were made
was still at work inspiring human toil,
to shape, and build, and trade, or till the soil.

I looked for Christ in Thaxted.
I sought him in the holy shrine
   where voice and instrument
 in music for his praise combine.
There, in the Word and sacrament, his grace
was present, with the glory of his face.

But when I meet in Thaxted
a childlike loving heart, and see
   a humble, faithful life;
 I need not seek, for Christ seeks me,
as once on man divine compassion smiled,
and sought us all incarnate in a Child.

September 1965

Now let us praise the names of famous men,
the poets of the sanctuary whose songs
gave, as the Spirit's breath inspired their pen,
a treasure that to every age belongs.
Those who have sung our Saviour's gracious Name,
or from the Psalmists' lines wrought Christian praise;
those learned in the ancient tongues, whose fame
is bright in hymns that generations raise;
from Ambrose and Aquinas, Luther, Keach,
to Watts and Wesley, Keble, Lynch and Neale,
and poets of this century who teach
us still the presence of our God to feel.
   In this imperishable heritage
   God gives his Spirit's grace to every age.

July 1966

Written at the suggestion of the Reverend Stuart W. Artless of Guildford

MORNING IN THAXTED

Morning in Thaxted brings a gift of joy
as I, early, rise to meet her,
in spring, the green blades piercing dark brown soil;
aconites beneath the beech tree,
cowslips and violets along the lane;
each eye delighting
to feel the warm enchantment of her kiss.
Larks flood the sky with music:
the bounding hare rejoices in a life
pulsing anew with spring's advancing sun.

Fragrant the gifts a summer morning brings
from rose, meadowsweet and hawthorn.
The corn is tall, with heavy ears inclined,
soon to fall before the reaper,
leaving but pale stubble, till autumn's fires
turn it to ashes;
while woodlands flame a farewell to the year.
Then winter's dawn brings off'rings;
crisp frost that gives each leaf a fringe of lace,
shadows from early sunshine on the snow.

Morning in Thaxted brings a wealth of joy
as I greet the early workers
and pass on with a silent prayer to bless
friends unseen within their dwellings:
or, on those dearest and most sacred days,
Christmas and Easter,
meet with them at the table of our Lord
to keep that blessed dayspring
when heaven's light dispelled a dark world's night,
bringing eternal sunrise to man's soul.

August 1966

TO A HOUSE-MARTIN

Released from a window

Vibrant with life, you lay within my hand,
one moment captive, that you might be free.
How hard it was for you to understand
that I who held you would deliverer be.
Your frantic wings beat on the window-pane
that shut you from the freedom of the air;
yet what your frightened struggles sought in vain
my grasp could give you with a moment's care.
Our human quest is freedom, and, like you,
we seek it wildly, seeing not the door:
until God grasps our life and bears us through
to his wide realm where we may freely soar.
      Fear not, my soul, his hand, so strong and wise,
      that frees your spirit for his boundless skies.

October 1967

A SONG FOR THAXTED

My song is Thaxted, ancient town,
by fields of corn surrounded;
upon a hill, in far-off years,
by men of Essex founded.
And when the Christian tidings came
to bless our English people,
to crown the little hill men raised
a noble Church and steeple.

While many generations passed,
the name of Thaxted flourished:
the cutlers and the weavers both
her fame and welfare nourished.
A Guildhall fair, and timbered homes,
their gift of beauty brought her:
for corn and wool and craftsman's work
men far and near have sought her.

Then music gave her joys to add
new wealth to Thaxted's treasures:
the merry Morris men began
with dance to swell her pleasures:
and in these ancient homes have dwelt
folk true in love and duty,
whose lives in ages past and now
are Thaxted's crown of beauty.

October 1967

101

LARK SONG IN THAXTED

The fields are full of song,
    cascade from heaven's secret springs of joy,
the skylark's salutation to the day,
in that fair season when green spears of corn
rise up to guard the young brood's tender life,
while yet the flaming sun
wrests from the darkness late and early hours.
Then, young birds safely fledged,
the sun's retreat begun, the song will fail;
and, as the bowed ears wait the reaper's stroke,
will die away until the fields are clear.
But when rich autumn splendour garbs the trees
lark song again will flood the skies with joy,
to herald that blest time when carols tell
how angel choir announced a holy birth
that promised earth more joy
than all the throbbing music of the skies
could ever bring to man.

October 1967

Wise Magi by a guiding star were led
    to Christ, with treasures for the infant King;
gold, frankincense and myrrh they came to bring,
in worship kneeling at his humble bed:
and now, though many centuries have sped,
the wise are still the same Lord worshipping:
they bring rich tribute and their praises sing
to him who humbly came this earth to tread.
We probe the skies today and space explore;
new galaxies and stars unnumbered find:
shall we, star seeking, find at last a door
that opens nature's secret to mankind?
A glory we shall, wondering, adore;
the hidden wisdom of creative mind.

September 1968

CHRISTMAS IN THE SPACE-AGE

'When I consider heaven', the Psalmist said,
   'Sun, moon and stars, created by God's hand,
what is mere man, that God has made him tread
the earth as lord of life in every land?'
Now man considers earth from space, a sphere
more beautiful to view than moon or Mars:
blue oceans, continents and poles shine clear,
a worthier home for man than countless stars:
and God has given a dignity to earth
beyond the ancient Psalmist's farthest ken:
he set his love's own seal on human worth
when Christ, his Word Incarnate, came to men.
   Now Christmas brings creation's word from space,
   and on the moon Christ offers man his grace.

September 1969

*On Christmas Day 1968 Frank Borman of Apollo 8 read the creation
story from space. Edwin Aldrin of Apollo 11 has described how he took
Communion on the moon*

MY CHRISTMAS VISION

Some poets write of agony and wrong
   marring our life in this strange world of tears:
the violence and cruelty of the strong,
men's hearts beset by evil, pain and fears.
Such is their vision, and I see it too,
I feel their pity and their anger share
that men should have such grievous ills to rue
and do this evil or its burden bear.
But I would tell how One from heaven came,
was born with cattle, snatched from tyrant's sword,
faced agony, betrayal, bitter shame,
but rose from death to be life-giving Lord.
   Lift up your hearts, sad poets of man's pain,
   for you the Christmas angels sing again.

August 1970

CHRISTMAS AFTER SEVENTY YEARS

S eventy years of Christmas,
   from those magic days
devised by parents' love
when Father Christmas visited a sleeping child:
   and carols, tree and games
   brought long-awaited hours,
   re-lived each year with joy.

Christmas Day in war years,
      mocked by human strife,
   the Prince of Peace dethroned:
yet still a lamp of love to men soon doomed to die;
   and reconciling sign
   to prisoners of war
   made welcome by their foes.

Christmas shared with races
      mingled at the Feast;
   prophetic of the Day
when men shall come from east and west to
      God's great realm:
   and Christ shall bring the world
   the peace that angel song
   proclaimed from God to man.

Seventy years of Christmas:
      still its glory grows
   as carols tell again
the ancient mystery of God's abode in man.
   The Lord incarnate comes
   to dwell in humble hearts
   and give the world his joy.

September 1971

FAREWELL TO THAXTED

It's Christmas now in Thaxted,
when, round the Guildhall tree,
folk young and old all gather
to celebrate with glee
the Child whose birth was destined
man's captive soul to free.
   Sing joy, sing life, sing love,
   join your heart's song
   with angel choirs above.

I shall not hear in Thaxted
the merry girls and boys,
or see the tree-decked windows
with fairy-lights and toys:
but I shall know the gladness
of all true Christmas joys.
   Sing joy, sing life, sing love,
   join your heart's song
   with angel choirs above.

In all the world it's Christmas,
so, everywhere, I hear
the tidings that gave shepherds
and Magi blessed cheer:
that in the Son of Mary
incarnate love drew near.
   Sing joy, sing life, sing love,
   join your heart's song
   with angel choirs above.

October 1972

CHRIST IN CHELMSFORD

When Thaxted's ancient loveliness I left
for Chelmsford, town of industry and trade,
I mourned for beauty lost, as one bereft
of treasures, art and craftmanship displayed.
Then, from my home, I saw, one Advent night,
amid the bright-lit office windows, clear,
a shining tower and pencil of pure light,
in silence telling of God's presence near.
As once the skies were bright with angel choir,
who carolled tidings of a Saviour's birth,
so now the glory of cathedral spire
proclaims the God who dwells with men on earth.
In workshop, office block and crowded street,
God's people still may their Deliverer meet.

March 1973

BRADWELL 1973

We came to Cedd's grey chapel on the wall
to share with youth the faith, hope, love and joy
of Christian people gathered to recall
the saint, and in God's praise the day employ.
From Lindisfarne eight sturdy pilgrims came
to greet the Bishop sea-borne to the creek.
In song we celebrated Jesus' name
and heard the call new lives for him to seek.
We shared our food, and then, with thankfulness
took bread and wine, Christ's body and his blood,
in fellowship, that he might life impart
and with his Spirit's love our being flood.
While, overhead, the larks God's glory sang,
as when Cedd's voice once through this chapel rang.

July 1973

GOD'S IMAGE

God said, 'Let there be light.'
The teeming particles
turned to ordered tasks,
forming the galaxies with myriad suns:
air, clouds and oceans paved the way for life;
then consciousness, and crowning all,
man in God's image came to rule the earth,
servant alone to his creator's will.

Man said, 'Let me be God.'
His restless energies
turned to seek base ends:
hatred and envy, greed, desire and pride
wrecked God's predestined harmony of man.
God's law and discipline were spurned.
Lost was God's image, or so far defaced,
vain seemed the hope that image to restore.

God said, 'I will seek man.
See my divinity
take a human face;
fashion anew the image man defaced.'
In Mary's child, discerned by shepherd eyes,
the bright epiphany appeared;
crowned by the Cross, love's perfect offering,
God's very image giving all for man.

August 1974

FENROTHER

The curving road ascends Longhorsley Moor
  past Gorfenletch, where once white foxes played,
till, just below the summit's distant view
of Cheviot and the steps of Simonside,
a lane turns eastward to the Great North Road.

There stands Fenrother Farm, its old grey walls
exposed to gales that sweep in from the sea
beyond the long line of Northumbrian shore:
a noble prospect on fair summer days,
but when the blizzards drive across the moors
a grim, forbidding scene, harsh to endure.

Yet in those walls the fellowship how warm,
when, gathered from the farms and cottage homes,
or ancient Morpeth town, the people came
to sing and pray and hear the Word divine.
Remembered scenes and voices throng to mind:
the farmhouse crowded for the Harvest Home,
hall, stairs and parlour loud with hymns of praise:
a tall, lean countryman in fervent prayer,
'Oh for that flame of living fire which shone
in Saints of old … On us thy Spirit pour':
that day when snow lay deep upon the roads
and traffic ceased, a preacher's gallant walk
from Stannington, eleven miles and back:
most precious memory of all to prize,
the quiet farmer and his gracious wife
whose welcome breathed the very peace of God.

So at Fenrother there is found today
that blest communion which in Christ unites
his Church on earth with all the host of heaven.

January 1975

*The Wednesday evening service at Fenrother Farm, the home of
the late Mr and Mrs Storey, originated from a Church Army Mission*

THE COST OF CHRISTMAS

I said –
   The cost of Christmas rises every year.
 The gifts, the post, the price of Christmas fare,
 and charities are asking more and more
 for hungry millions, aged, handicapped,
 the orphaned child, the man in prison cell.
 I must hold back, spare less for Church and friends,
 and keep enough for festive use and fun,
 to celebrate with fitting gaiety
 the birthday of the Holy Child.

God said –
   I paid the price of Christmas in my Son.
   I gave my love to you in him who came
   a peasant's child, in cave for cattle born;
   trained as a manual worker till he found
   a harder, costlier service on him laid,
   to bear the weight of human ills and sin,
   man's cruel hatred, violence and scorn
   upon the agonising, shameful Cross,
   that, pardoned, you might truly live.

I said –
   My Lord, enough! What gift can fully show
   I feel the measure of the debt I owe?

God said –
   Give me your life, that in it men may see
   a mirror of the love you saw in me.

July 1975

BIRTH FROM BIRTH

This day
  we celebrate an ancient birth,
  remembered through long years:
  God's love incarnate in a child,
  that we might learn to love like God.
  From that one birth unnumbered more
  have brought mankind new life;
  dead souls reborn to faith and hope and love,
  who found eternal joy through Jesus Christ;
  new births in knowledge and creative arts,
  new impulses to heal our human ills,
  to right injustices and shape this world
  according to the pattern of God's realm.

Lord, bring to birth in me today
  your gift of life,
  that through the year will grow,
  in faith and joy and power to create
  some work of beauty and enduring worth,
  a new compassion that will flow
  in tireless service to your people's needs,
  until my tasks for you, my Lord, are done.

August 1976

THE INNER VISION

I have seen beauty in the hills,
  on heather moors and alpine snows,
Orion mounting in the autumn night,
and white sea-horses racing for the shore;
the beauty of a rose, of gulls in flight,
and loveliness of human form and eyes;
the beauty born of man's creative thought
in matchless Parthenon, Giotto's tower,
or art of Michelangelo and Constable.

When age dims outward sight, give me, 0 Lord,
that inner vision which can see, within,
the beauty hidden from the outward eye;
an intellectual vision, to perceive
a beauty that the mind of Einstein saw
in laws uniting time and space
and energy and mass in ordered whole;
clear vision that imagination gives
the poet and musician, to create
a secret universe within the mind.

Give me love's vision most of all,
to see your greatness humble in a Child;
your glory in a Cross of pain and shame,
your mercy working through life's darkest hours
to bring me to eternal life and joy.
And in the light this inner vision lends,
help me to walk with you in humble love,
until all darkness ends, and I rejoice
to see the glory of your perfect day.

Teach me to see, through your own eyes of love,
the beauty hidden in the very heart
of every soul created by your grace.

September 1977

TO CYRIL TAYLOR ON HIS 70TH BIRTHDAY

When God gives seventy years,
he gives a wealth of time
for many gifts to grow and flower
and bear rich fruit
for Him, and for his people's joy.
You, Cyril, skilled in St. Cecilia's art,
have dedicated many years to him
whose birth was hailed with music by a heavenly choir.
Your life has tuned our voices for God's praise,
and taught our tongues to glorify his love.
Your gifts have called out gifts in other lives
to swell the chorus of the church's songs,
and add their offerings to her heritage.
Now we, your debtors, pray that you today,
with those you love, may know the fullest joys
of thankful recollections, and the hope
that God will still inspire your soul to song.

December 1977

*As one of many debtors, I recall that it was Canon Cyril Taylor's
discovery of my first hymn,* Rejoice O People, *in the L.M.S.
bookroom at Livingstone House, Westminster, leading to its
publication in* The BBC Hymn Book, *which encouraged me
to attempt further hymn writing*

ON HEARING THE SONG 'THE SKYLINE OF SKYE'

She sang of the skyline of Skye
the beautiful skyline of Skye,
and my thoughts took wing
over nigh fifty years
to the time I first saw
the wonderful skyline of Skye.

A fine Scottish pair bade me seek
the marvellous island of Skye;
there my eyes first looked
on the blue range of hills;
with their summits cloud-capped,
the jagged high Cuillin of Skye.

But storm-clouds swept over these peaks,
through Sligachan glen roared a gale,
and the burn in spate
was a peril to wade,
as I battled my way
to look upon fair Loch Coruisk.

I came with my love to Portree
to show her the skyline of Skye;
and by ev'ning light
as we walked side by side,
like a bright dream appeared
the magical skyline of Skye.

Together with joy we explored
the grandeur and beauty of Skye,
and beside a burn,
on a fair summer day,
with my palette in hand,
I painted the skyline of Skye.

Perhaps in a life yet to be
my spirit will venture to roam;
and I'll wing my way
to the isles of the west
to behold with new eyes
the glorious skyline of Skye.

April 1978

Written after the visit of a Scottish Group to
Christ Church U.R.C. Chelmsford

BEAUTY EXPLORED
Lichfield 1978

Three tall spires in the distance,
   seen from a passing train,
crown of an ancient city,
   now at last explored.

Pillars soaring in beauty
   up to a vaulted roof,
humour and skill of craftsmen
   wrought in wood and stone.

Choiring voices ascending,
   offering praise to God;
filling the house with glory,
   hearts with holy joy.

My first hymn of rejoicing
   echoed within these walls,
bidding God's people honour
   saintly lives of old.

Thanks I give to my Father
   bringing me now to stand
here in this house of beauty,
   long loved from afar.

September 1978

The first line echoes the first line of the poem
Beauty Unexplored

STAR-LED

Wise men, the ancient story tells,
were guided by a star to find a child
endowed with royal power
to show God's saving purpose for the world.

Today astronomers have seen
unnumbered galaxies and nebulae
and trace through long light-years
the birth and life and death of countless stars.

This process, they surmise,
began and ends in one dense fiery ball:
but man's exploring mind
discerns no purpose in the flow of change.

Yet in this process life was born,
and, crowning life, the child who, fully grown,
became astronomer,
and compassed in his knowledge time and space.

So child, astronomer and stars
are linked in God's age-long creative plan
to bring to birth his sons,
that they may know through Christ eternal life.

Now man again may be star-led
to learn God's cosmic purpose through a child:
the Child who grew to show
the glory of God's ways to all mankind.

October 1978

Suggested by the BBC Radio 4 programme Cosmos, *broadcast
on October 5th, 1978*

The hours are long, each day seems like a year:
we grope our way through corridor and ward.
Nurses and surgeon through a mist appear,
holding the promise of clear sight restored.

The sun is shining on the cricket ground
where Essex and Glamorgan fight it out,
and through an open window floats the sound
of batsman's stroke and keen spectator's shout.

The tide of active life around us flows,
but we are like an island off the shore:
and only one who waits here fully knows
the joy when loved ones enter at the door.

So pass the days until God's healing power
through human skill and care brings freedom's hour.

September 1979

OBERAMMERGAU 1980

Grey sky, a chilly air, a shower of rain,
for hours we watched the tragic theme unfold;
the shouting crowds with palms who hailed their king,
the Lord who cleansed the temple of its shame;
the darkening storm of anger round his head;
that upper room, where, with his chosen few,
our Lord's new covenant of love was made,
with bread and wine, his body and his blood;
his agony in dark Gethsemane,
betrayed into the hands of cruel men;
his trials and sufferings, the crown of thorns,
and that last dread ordeal upon the cross;
his body borne into the silent tomb.

Was that to be the end? It proved not so.
Creation and the Gospel answered, no!
The clouds were clearing, and the sun's warm rays
woke bird-song in the trees around the stage,
As Mary in the garden met her Lord.
With songs of triumph ringing in our ears,
we left the theatre for a quiet room
where, at a table bearing bread and wine,
we held communion with our living Lord.

August 1980

BORN OF GOD

A child was born of God
for Mary's joy
and for the joy of all the world.

Our love is born of God
if, as it grows,
the love of God fills our whole life.

All joy is born of God
which, shared, gives birth
to seeds of joy in other hearts.

True peace is born of God,
for Jesus Christ
bestows his peace upon his own.

All truth is born of God,
for truth itself
became incarnate in his Son.

True life is born of God,
eternal life,
the gift of Christ our risen Lord.

August 1980

ORION

Orion, glory of the winter sky!
My love would dance when first you rose each year,
and I rejoiced to view your majesty,
with belt and sword, and giant Betelgeuse,
bright Rigel and mysterious nebula.

The years moved on, town lights and clouded eyes
concealed your distant splendour from my sight,
and all your glory seemed remembered joy:
till, aided by a surgeon's skill, I viewed
God's universe with clearer eyes, and saw,
one Christmastide, your splendour shine again,
and with uplifted heart gave thanks to God
for shewing me once more his handiwork.

December 1980

HARVEST OF CHRISTMAS

I look upon the harvest of that life
through which God gave himself in humble love,
incarnate in the child of Bethlehem,
the carpenter and teacher, healer, Christ,
who, crucified, was buried like the grain
to rise and bear a harvest for the world.

This Bread of Life has fed me eighty years,
through Christian parents, teachers, faithful friends
and partnership in love creating home.

From God's rich harvest what seed have I sown
that he can use to feed the world to be?
He called me to proclaim and teach his love
and shepherd for him souls for whom Christ died.

His Spirit gave me songs to move his church
to voice her joy and penitence and prayer;
but only God's great harvest day will show
how many tares I mixed with his good grain.

I can but pray that he who showed his love
at Christmas, and gave all upon the Cross,
will give me mercy, and will find some seed
to grow new harvests in the coming years.

September 1981

JORDANS

The singer's voice soared high among the beams
of Jordans' ancient barn. The timbers spoke
of days when, strained and buffeted by storms,
they bore men's precious lives and merchandise;
and, so the learned scholar claimed, set sail
with one famed company of pilgrim souls
who sought a new world free from tyranny,
where conscience might be followed unafraid,
and God obeyed in all their common life.

Then, other voices drifted to the barn:
grave men were speaking of new sufferings;
one, Penn, proposed a great experiment;
a holy, peaceful, colony of Friends,
where persecution would be never known.
So, *Welcome* bore another pilgrim band,
to live in amity with Indian tribes,
and make new paths for people then unborn.

The barn was filled with songs of our own age,
that woke new voices growing to a choir.
They sang of pilgrims through the passing years
who launched love's enterprises round the globe;
to feed the hungry body, starving mind,
set free the pris'ner, house the refugee,
break down the walls dividing humankind,
and find new paths to lead the world to peace.

The singing ceased, the company dispersed,
one voice alone, the living Spirit, called—
'The future needs its pilgrims—who will go ?'

July 1982

*Jordans lies a mile east of Beaconsfield, Buckinghamshire. William Penn,
founder of Pennsylvania lived at nearby Penn. Penn's Quaker Meeting
House and the Mayflower Barn are at Jordans. Tradition has it that beams
used in the Barn were part of the 'Mayflower', the Pilgrim Fathers' ship*

ANCESTRY AND DESTINY

'Hosanna to the Son of David' sang the crowd,
proud of their nation's royal heritage
wherein this child of Mary took his place.
But David's ancestry included Ruth,
the Moabite whom Boaz took to wife:
and Abraham, the nation's founding head,
was rooted in the stock of Babylon;
while, first of all, came Adam, formed from dust,
yet called in Gospel record 'Son of God'.
Our common ancestry how lowly, but how great!

Now science, tracing human origins,
finds in a single cell the birth of life
and ancestor of all humanity;
a source as humble as the 'dust of earth',
rebuking all ancestral pride of race,
save that which every human being shares.
For God, who stamped his image on us all,
showed us his very self in human form,
the Adam of a new humanity;
that we, set free from bondage to our sins,
might bear at last his likeness, and become
the full-grown children of our Father's love.

September 1982

*These lines were sent as Christmas greetings to friends of
Albert and Grace in 1982*

SIMEON

Mine eyes have seen thy salvation   Luke 2.30

When aged Simeon held the infant Christ,
  he saw God's ancient promises fulfilled,
and even greater glory yet to come.
Long centuries have passed, and we have seen
the glory Christ has shed upon the world
in lives illuminated by his grace.
His saving light has spread from land to land,
and, as it dawned, new churches came to birth,
to grow and bear new lamps of truth and love.
The sick were healed, the prisoners released,
wrongdoers turned from evil ways to find
forgiveness and a life transformed by Christ.

All this we see, but much else clouds the hope
that heaven's glory will yet fill the earth.
Fear, hate and cruelty stalk the troubled world,
dark powers of evil strive to quench the light
which even in ourselves too dimly shines.
So we lose faith that God's love will prevail,
and hide his glory from our neighbours' eyes.

Forgive us, Father, our mistrustful hearts;
renew in us the vision and the faith
of Simeon, looking on the infant Christ;
that we may see your glory in his face,
and with our faith restored, receive your peace.

Written to celebrate Christmas 1983

Index of
First Lines and Titles

Index of First Lines and Titles

Titles of hymns and poems are shown in italic type
First lines of hymns and poems are shown in roman type